The Envelope System

Create your legacy through letters to your daughter

Dr. Brookh Lyons

Brookh Lyons

8/10/15

Today you have the gift of time.

Dr. Brookh Lyons

To bring a deeper connection with the importance of fathers, letters have been included by women who have lost their Dad. All of the letters that appear in this book are true stories as told by their author, and printed with permission. Otherwise, the names have been changed for privacy.

Author photo by Michelle Smith
Cover photo by Tara Day
Jacket and cover design by Strawberry Fields Design
Book design by Laurie Wheeler
Developmental Editor Dianne Campbell
Copy Editor Julie Rogers

Includes bibliographical references

ISBN-10: 1505572789
ISBN-13: 978-1505572780

Organizations may order in bulk by contacting our outreach department
Media@TheEnvelopeSystem.com

*This book is dedicated to every father and every daughter,
so that you may you find your way, together.*

CONTENTS

1

BEGIN HERE

You are important to your daughter ... to all of your children. However, because of the intrinsic and natural differences between girls and boys, many father-daughter relationships are difficult to navigate without a map. How can you make your thoughts known without pushing her away? Connecting with your daughter in a way that creates a loving relationship that flows through good times and bad is a must for both of you.

The Envelope System is a simple tool that will help you connect with your daughter, through letters. When you can communicate peacefully, it is simple for you to develop your relationship and build her up while also creating your legacy.

None of us know how long we have together. On the remote and unfortunate chance that you are pulled from her life too soon, that you are diagnosed with an illness or are facing the possibility of leaving her, whatever your circumstance, this is the time to prepare for her well-being. Your letters will provide your daughter with the stability and love you always intended her to have.

> *This is why The Envelope System is so*
> *significant, because you never know what*
> *the future holds and you simply must stay*
> *active and supportive in your daughter's*
> *life forever.*

NOTE: If you have been diagnosed with an illness, this is a time of great change for you. No one can imagine what it's like to hear the words you have heard and, until they are uttered, we never imagine they will ever be said to us.

And it's difficult to relate because no one can possibly know what you are going though. Each of us harbors various life experiences, hurts, and ideals that mire our ability to truly mull this over in a productive way. What **is** known is that YOU ARE IMPORTANT! And, in holding this book, you have the gift of time.

The Envelope System has been in the works for many years, but recently I became inspired when my friend, Dana, shared the sad news that her husband, Tim, was diagnosed with a terminal illness. We were all in shock and, while none of us can imagine what that really meant, we all understood the devastation the family was experiencing. Their whole life changed on a dime. Suddenly days were filled with appointments and difficult decisions. Not small decisions like what's for dinner or who is picking up the kids, but life-and-death decisions that affect the rest of their lives. In fact, we make so many important decisions mindlessly everyday about the foods we eat and the choices we make, but in the face of a terminal illness, all of the decisions start to stand out a little more.

And what about their daughter Megan?

It was on everyone's mind, and it was obvious to me that Megan simply MUST continue to have the influence of the most important man in her life. I couldn't contemplate her growing up without his input and his love, without the special way a father can challenge his daughter and help her grow to become confident and strong.

Truthfully, none of us knows when we will pass and most of us are not ready for it to happen, but it can happen in the blink of an eye. I think that when a diagnosis or injury comes with the possibility that we might leave our loved ones, it changes things. But not necessarily in a bad way.

It brings **focus.**

It also brings us the gift of **time.**

Twice in my own life, I thought I would die. It didn't happen, but the circumstances inspired me to ask many questions, and, most importantly, to think about ways to support my children if I were absent from their lives. No one expects their life to be interrupted, but with the way we eat and live these days, more and more people are in this tenuous position.

We all figure we have tomorrow and the next day to live our lives and impart our wisdom, to share feelings with loved ones, or maybe to repair fractured relationships or hurt feelings. The truth is you don't know how much time you have. No one does.

What we do know is that we get what we focus on. Focus on love and goodwill for your family, and it will come. Focus on health, and you'll head in that direction. You can focus on what you didn't do, didn't say, or how you missed the mark, OR you can put all your efforts into being exactly what your daughter needs to the very best of your ability.

Not all men will have the chance that you have today. Even great men who adore their wife and children are sometimes pulled away too soon. I would like to share a bit of the life of Adrian Mansbridge.

In creating *The Envelope System*, I searched for the perfect photo for the cover; something that would illustrate the beauty and necessity of that precious bond between a father and daughter. I reviewed many beautiful pictures.

One day the image of Adrian Mansbridge and his daughter, Ruby, came to my inbox. I instantly connected because it is simply breathtaking to witness such love and trust happening without words. But I could not thank Adrian for this lovely image. He had passed suddenly only months after the image was taken.

Adrian died at the age of forty-five without a warning, leaving a loving wife and three beautiful children younger than six. Life is not always fair, but Adrian's story is exactly why it is so important for each of us to write letters, establish our will and trust, and be prepared with the appropriate insurance, and all of the other things we do to prepare for the "inevitable," regardless of a terminal diagnosis.

In reading this book, you already have the greatest gift of all – TIME.

This gift of time is something Adrian and his family didn't get. Today you get to write letters to family members so that, no matter what happens, planned or by accident, you can be a part of your daughter's life for as long as she needs you.

This is a very selfless task. If you are ill, I know this is a tough time for you, but waiting or hoping for everything to turn out in the way you hope could leave your daughter without the most important male influence of her life -- YOU.

Even if you feel like you're a complete failure (*"I don't do enough;"* *"I'm not there enough;"* *"I'm a fraud;"* *"I don't provide well enough;"* *"I'm leaving behind my family;"* and so on), your daughter still needs you.

Throughout *The Envelope System*, many women have contributed their experiences about the loss of their own father. I hope you notice that each of the girls misses and needs her dad in much the same way. The letters are intended to encourage you, because indeed, your daughter needs you.

My father was a magician. His disappearing acts were quite frequent and, later, became permanent after he was imprisoned when I was seventeen. Many years would pass before I would receive a letter from him asking me for help. I was now forty-five years old, twenty-two years since I'd last seen him. After a massive heart attack, a triple by-pass, and the coming end of his prison term, I was faced with a decision. I offered this very ill, sixty-seven-year-old ex-con a place to live. This was tough. Bickering, shouting, laughing, crying, all of the emotions I begged for him to show me. The hurt we both felt smothered us. It was during this time that I really got to know him and he learned who his daughter really was. The hurt finally dissolved and we both embraced the love that was waiting for us. The trust, respect, and love began to grow. I fell in love with my father for the first time. And he finally fell in love with me. When he died at age seventy-five, the ending was magical. He was no longer the disappearing magician. He was my shining light.

I know, from the bottom of my heart, that if he had this book, The Envelope System, at the time when he needed it, it could have been the guide to use to start over and begin a relationship with his children, long before his death. I pray this book reaches the hearts of many fathers.

Debra

Choose to help her. And do it.

Many people believe we learn from our mistakes, and that can be true IF, (when we fail) we then see how things can be changed – and we change them. Within each mistake is a shred of something that worked. Show her that light; help her find what works.

The Envelope System helps you create emotional health for your child. Emotional health determines the choices we make and what we expect out of life. YOU always have hope and today, you can live on forever through the love of your child. Everything good about you will live on through her because she is yours and your letters will confirm your legacy.

Humans are great procrastinators, but today, you have the very special gift of focus and time. Accept your gift and make it productive. You ARE important to her and you are capable of showing your support and love toward your child, in every circumstance for as long as she needs you.

Prepare to be there for her – always. No matter what.

Throughout this book, you will read letters from real women who lost their father. Through their stories, you will know that communicating with your girl is important.

If you doubt your importance in her life, you have company. In a 2004 study, only thirty percent of fathers believed that active involvement in their daughter's life was vital to her health and well-being (Roper Poll, 2004). However, other studies done on the impact of the father-daughter relationship show that a father has a tremendous impact, influencing everything about his child. For your daughter, we are talking about everything from long-term male romantic relationships, views of the opposite sex, body image, sexuality, social skills and even academic success (Krohn &

Bogan, 2001).

And while most women interviewed believed they had loving relationships with their fathers, they believed the mother-daughter relationship was more communicative, more emotionally intimate, and more comfortable. Women wished their relationship with their father was emotionally and personally closer so they could more comfortably communicate about personal issues such as marriage, marital problems and divorce, drug and alcohol use, financial matters, depression, eating disorders, and sex before marriage (Nielsen, 2007).

The Envelope System is a series of letters you will write to your daughter. In your letters, you share your hopes, dreams, and positive influence while helping her become the most whole and healthy version of herself. If you've never really thought about that, you get what you plan for, so it will start you thinking about your direction as she grows. If you don't already feel like a positive or monumental influence in her life, your letters deliver this to your daughter in a gentle, and non-threatening way that will let her know that you truly care for her and want to be there for her.

For most girls, it's the special little things that matter most and that leads to a deeper level of trust and commitment. In your absence, your letters are everything. In your presence, they are reinforcing hope that leads to lifelong communication. In either case, it will create openness and love as you form a strong bond with the girl who needs and matters to you most.

The Envelope System is divided by chapters to give you ideas to help you tailor the contents of your letters to your own needs and the age of your child.

For ease of retrieval, place each letter in an envelope labeled with the subject matter and age in her life that is best for her to open the letter. You may choose to group your letters, for example, so her birthday letters are bundled together, or by age. You may think this is too much, but you are writing your notes one at a time. Some days you might get on a roll and write many, but remember that having even one letter is better than no letter at all.

One at a time ... you can do this.

Starting today.

Many people will benefit from your letters. (Think of those who made a difference in your life -- your wife, parents, friends, or others of great influence.) Just think about losing someone important to you. How many of us save one last letter from a parent, a grandparent, a friend, or relative just so we can see their handwriting and remember them? What would it mean to have a note written specifically for you from them explaining why they love you or reminding you about funny things you shared? Your words are valuable and will be powerful to share while you are still together! Women are complex and beautiful. To mature at her best, a girl's emotional side must be safe to explore, to learn, and to fail. You hold an important key.

The Envelope System is a universal system. It's not only for girls with fathers who are ill. Every girl, indeed every child, wants to know their parents. Every daughter wants her father to communicate his wishes and dreams for her life. She wants proof, provided in a way she can understand, that she matters to you.

In the case of a terminal diagnosis, the opportunity to have time to share our selves with our kids is rare and special. When I thought I would not be here for my children, I created letters for them and for other loved ones -- just in case. Making the connection between what we want to provide for our children and what they truly need from us provided the answer to the query:

How can your presence be everlasting?

You can do it through personal letters from you to her.

Writing letters about your life connects you at a deeper level than most of us currently are and, even if you are not ill, preparing these letters will give you peace of mind, knowing she will never totally lose you. You will pass eventually, but you will forever live on through your letters and she will know you gave great thought to how her life would unfold. Imagine what security and confidence that would bring, knowing that from your own parents.

It is that type of connection that makes for stable and emotionally connected adults. Even if you didn't get that growing up, or you are not confident you can do that now, you CAN provide security for your children. *The Envelope System* will show you how.

"The bond between father and daughter is one of the strongest in the world ... [and] if the father and mother are the right role models, the daughter will grow into an independent young woman." (Norment & Chappell, 2003)

Author's Note

To the Fathers reading The Envelope System

This book is meant to inspire you to write letters to your daughter to create a legacy of love. She wants to know you. She wants to know that you love her and know that you think she is pretty, smart and capable, and that you are proud of her. Focus on the positive. You are about to learn simple ways to say and write things so that you will be heard by speaking in a way she will understand. This does not require more force; it requires your time and commitment to the simple process of writing her notes. When she needs reinforcement, your letters will remind her how much she is loved. It's truly just that simple.

Relationships can be tough, so whether or not you are right there beside her, she will miss you and it will be a way to keep you close.

If you are ill, turn over every stone. Search for what is working in health care and seek health and healing. There is ALWAYS hope.

Planning always leads us in a stronger direction. It starts with you and your girl. Show her that you are concerned for her life.

It is with sincere gratitude that I thank you for letting The Envelope System be a part of your journey. I pray for your health, health in your relationships, and that your children grow up with confidence, self-esteem and strong character, knowing they are loved by you.

With your letters, your will live on forever.

Bless you,
Brookh

2

Plan to Succeed

I know we've talked a lot about your letters being important "just in case," but when you can connect with this possibility, your letters to your girl will deepen and become more important and life boosting. If a loved one has passed from your life, you know the questions left unanswered and the words left unsaid, so let's begin there.

> "I wish I had said this or done that."
> "Too bad I didn't tell her I love her more often."
> "I wonder if he loved me."

These are all normal questions that come with great loss. But studies show that most young girls have the same unanswered questions about their LIVING father.

Right now, you have the gift of time to take those questions and any possible regrets out of your life's equation. You can leave a legacy of strength and love when you create something physical and tangible that will be with your child, your daughter, forever.

The male-female relationship can be somewhat of a mystery to many people, and this includes the father-daughter relationship.

The Envelope System includes letters that you will write to her. Breathe! It's no big deal to write them, but it's a HUGE deal that you DO!

Your letters don't need to be fancy. They can be as simple as notes written in bullet points. This book will provide you guidance but feel free to write the letters in any way that works best for you. There are, however, several girl-guidelines in the following chapters to help assure your daughter receives the information in the very best way. You will even learn about the top five letters that women of all ages would like from their dad.

No more guessing.

This system is bound to bring you peace and calm in the midst of any frustrations, regrets, or guilt that you might be feeling. It also will bring you peace of mind, knowing that you are planning for her life and are able to let her know your thoughts and ideals. Your letters WILL influence her positively for the rest of her life.

Your personal life triumphs and failures can empower your children when they realize that both are totally normal and to be expected during the course of a lifetime. Your children really want to know you and to feel that you love and cherish them. This is a great way to make sure that happens.

"ANY IDEA, PLAN, OR PURPOSE MAY BE PLACED IN THE MIND THROUGH REPETITION OF THOUGHT."
-Napoleon Hill

The following are ideas to get you thinking about what this means to you and what it will mean to your daughter. Each person has different goals and thoughts so the messages are never the same. But let me encourage you to be everything she needs: loving and caring. Cherish the person she is and see her beauty that shines just because she is who she is. All girls want acceptance by the single most important man in their life, their father.

We all benefit greatly from setting clear expectations and knowing when we are meeting those expectations. Your child needs to know what you think, specifically what she is doing correctly. Certain learning and life skills will help her succeed, so what are those traits? Encourage her to work hard, set goals, and know her own heart. She has dreams and ideas. Let her know that THOSE are hers to nurture and grow, and that she is perfect.

This is a good idea for you as well. If you find yourself bashing your letters in any way, stop and remember that even one letter is more than you had to offer before taking this on.

When she knows that she is perfect just the way she is, and loved for just being herself, your daughter will strive for the very best in life because she clearly sees that goodness IS a possibility. When you point a finger at her weaknesses or tell her she's a certain (negative) way, it helps seal her into that negative notion. Set her free by only using specific, positive praise with your pure love and adoration.

All people benefit from having clear expectations and knowing when they are meeting those expectations. If you can share specifically what your daughter is doing correctly then she will focus on those and be more successful.

Questions to answer first:

Finding my Focus

- Why am I doing this? How do I want to help her? What do I want the outcome or final result to be? How do I want her to think about me? To think about herself? Write your answers then close your eyes and image the goodness of what that looks like. Write that down, too.

Plan of Action

- Document how you will execute your new mission to create your legacy. Include your goals and dates of anticipated completion. Focus keeps us on track. Continually update this document to keep it current.

- Constantly revisit your goals, dates and focus. It will keep you moving toward your target.

- When will I write? TIP: Pick a consistent time of day to work on this. You can write anytime, but consider choosing a specific time and stick with it as often as you can. You can certainly write at other times, but consistency is important in any successful model.

- How many letters will I write? What is my deadline for the letters? TIP: Committing to a specific date that you will have the bulk of your letters written also encourages your success. A letter a day is a great way to begin.

- How will I present my letters to her? TIP: Consider what is best for both of you. You may offer the letters in one big box so she can open them at her choosing or when she's ready. Or give them to her as your lives progress together. It really depends on your situation and how many letters you write. This could become a lovely tradition, one that she will cherish, knowing her dad took the time to make sure she is taken care of just in case he couldn't be there. It could also be a fun bonding experience as you reread the letters you wrote long ago, guessing what she would be like in future years.

- You must remember this is a GIFT to her, and you can have no expectations about what will happen.

- Will she open the letters? Probably. However, WHEN will she open them is the big question. Do not expect anything in return – nothing at all. She must process it on her own. Your letters will help her face whatever comes in her life, and encourage her to process every situation well so she walks through life with strength.

This information is especially important if your relationship is strained. Let her build her strength; give her the freedom to choose. In doing this, you will be rewarded in ways you've never dreamed.

Throughout this book, there are various letters written by women who have lost their fathers to illness. They share their experience, hoping their stories will help you know how important it is for you to communicate with your loved ones. Each woman says letters would have changed everything. Their fathers can't make it happen anymore, but you can.

The Envelope System is such a gift, such a tool for all those experiencing major life changes that might possibility lead to having to say goodbye to loved ones, especially close family.

My story began when I was sixteen years old and living in London, UK, with my Mom and Dad. My older sister had already left home, so it was just my parents and myself living together in the family home. At sixteen, I first came into close contact with the reality of cancer, for it was then that my Dad was diagnosed with colon cancer, and had the first of several procedures and operations.

When I was born, my Dad was a serving police officer, constantly working night shifts, so my Mom was home with us on her own most of the time. When I was three, my Dad was seriously ill with meningitis and nearly died. He had to go into a convalescent home for six months to recover. These early years, when my Dad was not around much, meant that he and I did not really get a chance to bond together as a father and daughter should. My dad was an intelligent, wise, and creative man, yet I was unable to really communicate with him.

I think that a reason for this was my experience before I was born. I had a twin brother with me who died early on while we were both still inside my mother's womb. It was a very traumatic experience, which affected me very much. To influence this further, my parents were not aware that there were two of us in the womb. I was born with pre-verbal trauma and no one knew. As a young baby, my Mom told me I use to rock my cot so violently each night that it would move from one end of the room to the other. It took me many years to resolve this prenatal trauma and come to peace.

All these early experiences, I know, affected my relationship with my father. It wasn't until the year before he died of advanced-stage cancer (when I was twenty) that we became close and began to communicate with each other in a more connected way.

And then he was gone. I was devastated. I loved my father so much and wanted our new friendship to have time to deepen and grow. Sadly, this was not to be.

Through all my life experiences since then, I so often wished I could have had my Dad with me to give his wise advice, laugh with me, be proud of me, and share with me stories of his life. If only The Envelope System had been available then, I would have loved and benefitted greatly to receive letters written to me before he died.

If you are a father or parent of a child, I wholeheartedly encourage you to take full advantage of this wonderful tool. I send you and your family all my love and blessings for cherished and precious times together for as long as is possible. Peace Be with You.

Janice

Writing Tips

Read each Tip; It matters

Consider the following when thinking about your daughter and what she needs from you in your letters.

Be specific.

According to research, saying "you are a smart girl" is not as powerful as being specific and saying "you did a good job reading" (Kamins, Dweck). While there are worse things to say than you are a smart, you are pretty, or you are talented, unless your meaning is specific, your girl may not understand clearly and interpret and use your words as powerfully as you hope.

Also, humans naturally strive toward goals (Ferguson 1984). But there is one thing more that we all strive for in creating our life. Depth. Maslow's called it his "Hierarchy of Needs" and describes it as words that are positive and specific. Guide her toward what she is doing right and she will seek to do that more often.

- I urge you to hand write your letter, if it's possible. I have recipe cards from my grandmother and the cards are so special because they are all written in her cursive handwriting. The writing is beautiful. Seeing her handwriting and holding the cards makes me feel closer to her. It also serves as proof that she cared enough about these particular recipes to write them out. They were hers. She made them. She touched them! They are also stained with the ingredients she used, and that makes me love the cards even more.

- Write through your tears. Smile with the memories. Draw strength in knowing that, through your daughter's eyes, you are changing the world and how she lives the rest of her life. This affects her, and your grandchildren, and generations to come.

- Bad things happen to everyone and your input about how to deal with that is important. Write about the lessons you've learned through such experiences. Include something you wish you'd done better so she can learn from the situation.

- Stay positive. It's OK to write ABOUT negative things because that's real life. If you have been diagnosed with a terminal illness, I am sure your diagnosis is the biggest and most negative thing either of you have ever dealt with. Sharing some of your thoughts about it is huge, but in a positive way that will help her understand. Tell her you really want to be there or to have a closer relationship. She will understand that through your letters.

- In each of your letters be sure to describe your experience using who, what, why, where, and when. Maybe you think it's girlie to be this descriptive, but remember these letters are not for you. They are for your daughter and girls like a full description and want to know as much as possible (we want to know everything when possible).

- The prettiness of the package is never what's important. Yes, most girls love a pretty package. In this case, however, it's more important that you write these letters for as many occasions as possible. You can use pretty stationery or basic lined white paper, but to be honest, that is not what matters. Your words and what this means is what it is all about.

- Having your letters of kindness and consideration validates her and tells her that she's OK just the way she is. It also gives her the strength to change in ways she needs to so she can accomplish what's in her heart. But you can't tell her to change. She must come to it on her own. Your support and love will help her get there. Again, focus on what she's doing right so she directs herself towards that.

- It's OK if you have to dictate your entries because you are too exhausted or unable to write. Tape yourself and have someone type the recordings into letters so she has something to hold. Then sign each printed letter so she sees it as your work. Also, be sure to leave the recordings as well as the envelopes with the letters – what an extra special gift to hear your voice! She will love seeing or hearing you talking or singing. Do you like to whistle? All of those will be things that one day she will wish she could hear one more time. My Grandpa used to whistle all day long. Sometimes I think I hear him, and how I wish I had recordings so I could.

- Labeling your envelopes is important. Include the current date, topic of the letter and the appropriate life event or age that she should open the letter. Write for whatever age or stage calls you to put your words on the paper. When finished, mark the contents and age or time of her life when she is best to open the letter to make sure all your effort is used in the very best way possible and your daughter will open your letters when appropriate or as needed. More importantly she can revisit them as often as she needs.

- Look for the positive. Communicate the positive. Be specific.

- Feel free to cut photos from magazines. I have an envelope full of images that represent various life events and emotions. This will help you focus your thoughts on those events where she may want your input but you can't quite picture her in that situation yet. This may require some imagination, the coming chapters will guide you.

- You also can use photos of your daughter or other loved ones as inspiration. Be sure to include a copy of the inspirational photos with the letter in the envelope to help her connect in a deeper way.

- There are no rules, just love and a life to be shared. Was there someone special in your life who left you when you were young? Do you ever wonder what they might have said in various circumstances if they were here? Write about that. How might they react in moments of success – or maybe in times of need? Answer those same questions for your child. This is what you are offering your daughter so she is never alone and wondering what you might have to say.

The opportunity to know what you think, and how you feel about things, is good for her life as well.

So sit and think about her life's events: new schools, sports, jobs, learning to drive, prom, graduation, relationships, marriage, etc. Imagine all that goes along with these events. With graduations, for example, consider the event, the dress, the parties, the "after parties." It will be very emotional -- just write and share your heart.

REMEMBER...

Please...remember one very important thing in this process. Try NOT to tell her what to do. Instead, guide her by using your experience or experiences as an example.

When you recount an event or a personal experience, just tell the story. Your child will hang on every word; she will "get it" and understand your message.

Be descriptive. If you like a certain holiday or season, or the way the tree is decorated at Christmas, explain why. Is it the lights? Is it the memories of childhood or a feeling that stuck with you? Did you have a tree growing up? Was that special? What makes the experience worth sharing with your girl?

DO include the tough stuff because difficult life events could well be the time when she needs your input the most. If she has an envelope labeled, "When Life Sucks," she will read it because the real things in life are what trip us up and are when we need the most support. Even the most independent girl wants a variety of feedback to shape her decision. Let her have the freedom to know your perspective, even if she chooses not to follow your guidance. But what if she does?

Remember that our difficult moments can bring the best learning. Tell her about those trying times in your life. If you are writing about your least-liked high school teacher, it's relatable because she most certainly has one, too! Your thoughts, actions, and experience might make her laugh, but it also will help her learn to deal with it. Honesty is good. Your wisdom is good, too. Sharing how you felt then and how you feel about it now can be a life lesson without her even knowing it is one.

We all face many struggles in our lifetime. You have experienced things and, without a doubt, you learned something through it. Did you move forward with the gift of experience and the best the situation had to offer, or did you take on anger and resentment and let it affect your future experiences? It's fair to say your child will face challenges as well, and, just as the muscles of your body must be exercised to grow, she will need to practice and experience things in her own life to prepare for success. Share your tough moments and describe the situations that taught you the most. Include things like what you might have done differently. What would you have changed if you could go back? What did you take from it moving forward in your life?

Writing a letter about your own experience is a powerful way to teach your daughter because children learn more from what we do than from what we say. That can be a good thing if we learned something good to pass on. She wants to know the real you; she is part of you and will likely feel or do many of the things just as you do, so help her by being your true and authentic self. She will honor and love you for who you are – no matter how imperfect you may feel about things. Your letters will provide the strength and courage you might not have been able to share otherwise.

Women long to be loved, nurtured, appreciated, taken care of, and protected. Your letters will do all of that. She will feel cherished.

Lastly, remember that *The Envelope System* offers you a guide to many of life's moments where you can plan and support her no matter how long you have together. The following chapters contain idea lists to get you rolling and keep you on track, but if a question in the book reminds you of something that is not on the list, please, WRITE it, or record it on tape or video! This is your legacy. Share what you think is important for your loved ones to read. It is all yours!

3

What she wants to know

In Daughter's Focus Groups, the question was asked: "What are the most important things you want to know from your father in order to help you navigate your own life with more ease and peace? What do you need to hear? What needs to be done? What do you want to KNOW from your DAD?" The group included young girls and grown adult women.

The women came from all walks of life, all different backgrounds – some from dysfunctional families and others from very loving, caring and nurturing families. What is amazing is that each woman agreed – no matter their age -- that these are things they want to hear from their dads! If you have little time to write, or when you are stuck, come back to this list. It will give you direction and inspiration. Keep it simple.

She Wants to Hear, Read, KNOW THIS from YOU

- I love you

Say I love you often, do things to show your love, and write the words so she can read them when she needs to. While it is great to say nice things about personality and look, how she dresses, or to give her gifts for no reason, "I love you" and "I'm proud of you" tied as the <u>No. 1 Most Powerful Thing</u> a dad can say to his daughter.

As soon as possible, square your body softly to your daughter, look her in the eye with a big smile and say the words as gently and as kindly as you can, "I Love You". Do it daily. This moment- where you stop time to focus only on her is enough to change everything in your relationship.

It is enough.

- I'm proud of you

Be specific so she KNOWS why you are proud of her. Is it just because she's yours, because she is capable of good things? What are those good things? Is it about you and your feelings or her and her uniqueness, or both? Say it, and say it often, because you ARE proud of her, and you are OFTEN proud of her! Knowing that will help her.

- Share words of wisdom

A dad is wise. You have been through things, seen things, and know first-hand about the land of boys. All girls want to be adored and protected (even if she doesn't want to look like she believes that, or if tensions of the past have developed a lack of trust; today is a new day). Talk to her about all the things she will have to manage in her life ... boys, sex, or abstinence, partying, trying drugs or any of those types of things that are peer-pressure based. Also, dating, marriage, what men look for and need in their wife, parenting, career choices, and the list goes on and on. I know I said earlier not to tell her what to do but it is worth repeating – you are not telling her what to do or not to do. You are sharing your thoughts regarding the choices she can make and what you see as the consequences (good or bad) of those choices. Remember that you are sharing your thoughts because you love her and care about what happens in her life. Please understand that she may not choose your suggestions, but your input is a part of how she will gather ideas to create her own decisions, so she must know what you think.

This is a great time to include your morals and beliefs so she knows what you're thinking, and perhaps, will choose the same path.

- **I'm sorry**

What can you specifically say you're sorry for? She will learn a lot from your apology, including that it's OK to be truthful and admit that we all make mistakes. Even unintentional mistakes deserve an apology. Your acknowledgement of things that you did not intend for could set her free. Does someone else need your apology? If there is a need to, just say you are sorry and share it from your heart.

This might not be an apology to your daughter, but knowing how you felt about the situation at hand and why you apologized will help her to swallow her pride one day and choose peace, even if it's not easy or, possibly, that her apology is not even well received. You will help her do the right thing even when it's difficult.

- ## You (My Girl) Are Important

Women wonder whether we are important. We don't always feel important. Often times we struggle with that feeling and sometimes we decide that the most horrible lies about us are true. Lies told by our parents when they are hurried or stressed. Things like we are too slow, too stupid, or can't do something right. The list is exhaustive and you can probably identify with your own thoughts as well. Your daughter has them, too. In fact, it has been said that a girl hits the peak of her self-esteem at the age of nine! By then she has learned about her value by the circumstances around her. This is not a time to lament in this fact; it is a time to do something positive to help her.

Girls, like women, worry about their grades, friends, activities and "am I pretty". She wants to be a good person, a good mom, a good wife, worker, and lots more. Life can be stressful. A letter about worry would be good for anyone because worrying is a terrible pastime that only creates more drama in our lives. Drama does not help make a powerful and wonderful life but, in order to be at peace, a woman must have supportive friends and family who help her be strong and seek positive experiences and positive people.

Also, women talk things out. This is why every man should encourage the women in his life to have girl friends with whom to talk. Men often misinterpret a girl's willingness to talk as the man-code for "help me" because if a man asks a question, he usually wants an answer. That's not the way girls work, not usually anyway. This difference can change her life because, if you tell her to relax or chill-out when she must express these thoughts to be able to process the situation, she will feel, at best, misunderstood.

Encourage your daughter to find supportive, positive people to talk with since her natural tendency is to gather as much information as she can (girl-style) to make a decision. Help her understand who to go to, how a man reacts in these situations, and how you feel when girls want to talk about their emotions. She needs to know.

Help her "get it" and, by the way, you may not "get it" and that's OK. No one really does.

Try to imagine what your daughter goes through at any age. To hear from her dad that she is important is more powerful than you will ever, ever know. Be THAT voice. Give her wings to fly with confidence and surety that she truly is ... Important.

Also, if you fear not having much time to write, most women agree that a note to read on her birthday is special, so consider writing a simple note, including a Happy Birthday wish, for several years to come. For example, write a letter for each of the next five consecutive birthdays as well as one for every five or ten years after that.

In case it's tough for you to image your daughter in the future, I've provided notes from Tanja, a woman who lost her father when she was a little girl. She began writing notes to him to share her life and to feel close to him. Through her notes, she feels connected. This is the same power your notes will have when your girl reads them, but they will be from you, sharing the answers to the questions that Tanja can only ask.

You will see more of her notes as the book progresses.

Turning 16

Dad,

I'm turning sixteen today. Happy Birthday to me! I miss you so much and really wish you were here. I'm supposed to get my driver's license soon, but I really don't want to. I'm not sure why. Mom is trying to teach me to drive and is doing a good job, but I just don't feel comfortable with the stick shift. I think I'm going to wait a while. What do you think?

-xo

If you have more than one child, it's OK to write a similar letter to each, but remember they will probably compare. If you are short on time, copy the letter, but if possible, change it a bit for each child. Bundle the letters separately for each child. There are many options here.

ONE LAST REMINDER

REMEMBER most importantly that you are talking to a girl, your little girl (even if she's fifty years old!) Girls don't think like you. You cannot tell her what to do or how to do it and don't be offended when she doesn't follow your exact advice. She is a talker, listener and a gatherer -- a girl. Give her examples, tell her a story and she will extrapolate from your words what she needs to make her decision.

You have the tools.

4

Directions

First, you need supplies. Remember your letters do not have to be on fancy stationery – they can be on simple lined paper. The paper can be different each time. HOWEVER, each letter MUST have an envelope explaining the letter's contents and the appropriate age when she should open the envelope and read your letter. Have a supply of envelopes on hand. Bundle your letters together by age range or topic so she can easily retrieve as needed.

Each chapter in this book is written for different ages and stages of your daughter's life. Each age group includes instructions and ideas about her possible thoughts for this particular time in her life. You may find some of it repetitive as you progress through her years. *The Envelope System* is designed this way. You might revisit a topic repeatedly as you find there are many things to share at different ages about a particular topic. You might skip a topic at one age and find it makes more sense at another age. Remember there is always something about which you can give positive praise. And if you can't find it, look harder.

Eventually you will reach a point in the book that is more event-specific. Think about your daughter's journey through life, on her way to becoming an adult. You can't know at what age she will decide to get married, have children, or even buy a house. For that reason, the book moves into things you know (or hope) will happen in her life.

LETTER CONTENTS:

What to Include

IN YOUR LETTER:

Dear......

     (body of the letter)

I am always with you (or your favorite salutation, maybe include her nickname? Or a joke, something that connects the two of you in joy.)

Love, Dad

Your ideas will build as you write. Write whatever letters you feel passionate about as you take pen in hand. The ideas in *The Envelope System* are suggestions to use in whatever way are best for you and your daughter.

What To Include

ON THE ENVELOPE:

1. Her AGE or Topic Level. For example - Your Eighteenth Birthday, High School, Getting Married, etc. Be specific so she knows WHEN to open the letter.

2. The TOPIC that you have chosen to write about. For example – Show Choir, Boys, What I Love About Your Mother, etc., so she knows what she will be reading about.

3. Sign in the bottom right corner - Love, Dad

Each envelope includes both the age or life phase when she can open the letter along with the topic of information for easy retrieval. You are on a journey of projected life with your daughter as she matures into the woman you know she can be, so ... here's a bonus:

4. BONUS * Be kind and respectful, always.

   There is NO ONE in the world about whom you may bash or speak unkindly. Relationships change and humans tend to identify with pain more than pleasure. Bashing people will not teach her how to succeed in life. Your job is to create your legacy and be sure she has every tool to succeed.

Read through the entire book first. *The Envelope System* will help you become more comfortable with the process and how to communicate better with your girl. Then, either write as you feel led, or go to the chapter in this book that is the current age of your daughter. Grab your pen, paper, and an envelope, then re-read the corresponding section and begin writing.

If you are feeling unsure or out of your comfort zone, I recommend you start with a Letter of Introduction – let her know what this is about and how weird it might be for you to be doing this. She might also find it weird to be receiving these letters, so put her at ease, and let her know your thoughts about the process. Let her know your emotions about your own situation; tell her how much you love her and that your intention is to be with her throughout her life no matter how long you have together.

Also, as you begin to write more, you may find that you have things you want to add to the completed letters. I suggest you keep a notebook, jot those notes down and share those sentiments by simply adding the notes to the letter. Re-writing takes time away from writing new letters and everything is a lesson. Adding a note teaches her that life is not perfect and thoughts are developed. Feel free to add and change as the situation requires. For this reason, you may choose to leave the envelopes unsealed. Ask a trusted confidant to seal them in the event of your passing, or just leave them open.

As inspiration, cut photos out of magazines or use photos of your daughter or of your life. Include the photo with the letter so she can visualize what you are writing about.

It does not matter if you write one paragraph or one page. What matters is that you write, expressing what you want to say and always saying it with love. Even if your pages are sparse in the beginning, they will fill. It will become a natural transition for you to go from not knowing what to write to wanting to write every day! Writing is a great way to process emotions and to gain focus. She will learn from your thoughts and experiences. Share words that will help her understand you better. Be honest with her, apologize if you need to, celebrate her momentous times, and most importantly, be authentic. Always use your own words, although you can use quotes as inspiration or to summarize an idea.

Pretend you are having a face-to-face conversation with your daughter. Express your mannerisms; share what look you might be giving her, what tone you might be speaking in, or how big your smile is as you celebrate her life. You might include a photo of you smiling at the camera in each letter of celebration so she can see your proud and wonderful face. She will never tire of the same photo. She WANTS to see you.

Always come from a place of love, support, and unconditional admiration. She will always need that from you – she is a GIRL! Even a simple, "I love you, you can do it!" is absolutely fine! Write it down and seal it up in the envelope!

Here is an example:

Let's say your daughter is six years old and in first grade. But NOW your task is to imagine her in the future, as a teen. Imagine her as a thirteen-year-old -- a teenager. What are your hopes for her? How do you feel about her? You are writing to her about life lessons she will be introduced to at that age and your envelope needs to let her know that.

A Sample Tween Stage Envelope

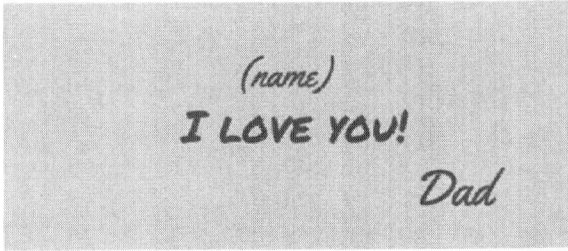

You have everything you need simply by drawing from your own personal life experience. It's time to write some letters.

If you procrastinate, remember the true story of Adrian Mansbridge who died suddenly at the age of forty-five and begin your letters now.

5

Before BIRTH to age 9

A lot happens from the minute you find out you will be a father, to the birth of your daughter and on to age nine. Your child arrives in the world completely dependent on those around her for her care and very existence. By age nine, she is capable of so much more. Every day she is maturing through the experiences of her life in the way she thinks, the way she looks at the world, and how she acts within her circumstances.

There is a lot of research available online if you want to look into this more, as well as a multitude of books on the subject, but today let's focus on the simple fact that your girl is growing up and this is a time of great need for your child. She is not capable of being on her own, but she is becoming more independent and learning specific things through experience. Whether intended or not, this is the time when she will develop many negative thoughts about herself and when those negative things will be confirmed in her immature mind through her experiences. This happens to all of us, regardless of our upbringing.

Kids learn more from what you do than from what you say, but if you contribute to her life with your wisdom and thoughts, a girl grows up knowing that she is loved and cherished. This can help her in many ways. Your letters show that you care about her life, that you are sensitive to her needs, and that you know she is, and will continue growing into one super fantastic beautiful human, living life in the best way she knows how. With your support, your letters will help her develop so she is better equipped to become her best.

When you provide her with those things, she will seek a partner who also provides that security, safety and love. Your job as a father will be a success.

Sample Envelope Label

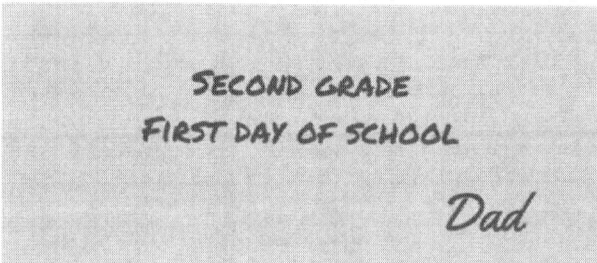

SECOND GRADE
FIRST DAY OF SCHOOL

Dad

Letter Ideas

CHILD

REMEMBER girls love description and details, so include who, what, where, why, when, and how in your letters. (I know, I sound like your fourth-grade English teacher!)

There is simply SO much to write about through this first phase of growth. The following are ideas. Go with it and start writing.

When You Were Born

When Your Mom Told Me She Was Pregnant

What You Were Like As A Baby

What You Were Like At Age 1, Age 2, Etc.

Your Very First Boo Boo, Step, Tooth, Etc.

Teaching You How To Ride A Bike, Swim, Skate, Etc.

Your First Day In Pre-School

Your Artwork From School

You Are My Pretty Princess

Faith And Family

Things We Like To Do Together

What I Treasured Most About Your Childhood

What Funny Things You Did As A Kid

Respecting Yourself and Others

Why I'm So Proud Of You

Why I Love You/What I Love About You

Why You Are So Special To Me

My First Crush

What I Loved About Grade School

What School I Went To And What It Was Like

How I Got To School (Bus? Walk? Driven?)

My Favorite Music, Movies, Books, Etc.

What Did I Participate In/ What I Wish I Had Participated In

What I Did Well In School

What Were My Priorities?

What Was Considered Really Bad When I Was A Kid?

Where I Lived In Grade School (include the address so she can visit someday)

What I Loved Or Didn't Love About Grade School

All About My Friends (mention if you have lasting connections)

I Believe In…

I Am Most Grateful For….

Funny Things Adults Did Back Then

6

Tween – ages 10 to 12

Tweens are not kids anymore, but they are not ready for all that teenage stuff either, although they truly believe they are! Middle childhood is a time when your child will move into a wider range of social contexts that greatly influence their development.

This is a very vulnerable time for your daughter and your effort is going to be impactful toward her self-confidence and self-esteem. A girl of this age is not yet equipped to know what is meant by constructive criticism. She is extremely sensitive, (and will continue to be throughout her lifetime), even if she does not show it to the outside world. If you have a keen and watchful eye, you will see it. You must use Specific Positive Praise so she can focus on moving toward the good of her life. Some girls will take on the negative words they hear (either words said to them directly or those they imagine they hear) as being the truth about themselves and live life true to those words. She might believe and own that she is "bad stock" and not deserving of love or anything good in life. Girls who develop respectful relationships, effective communication and spend time with their parents believe in themselves. They are strong, confident, and able to handle negativity in a better way.

When you write, find your "funny" – deliver your stories and the lessons within them with humor, especially laughing at yourself, although not in a way that is insulting to you. In our focus groups, girls of this age want to hear funny things from their dads. Your girl might be more serious, but a commonality among all girls is that they just want to feel safe. School is getting harder, social pressures are getting tougher – there is a lot of drama happening. Your ability to laugh, share knowledge, tow a strong line of parenting mixed with love and respect will help her navigate this stage easier.

It is always important that she hears the words "I Love You", "You're Perfect Just The Way You Are" and "You are pretty."These phrases are important at this stage of growth and keep on saying them throughout her life. Perhaps this will be the most difficult time to say those words if you have a very independent, challenging daughter. If that's the case, the argument can be made that this is the time where your love and stability is needed most. You might want to say many other, perhaps negative, things to her, but don't. It is normal for our kids to push their boundaries and to learn to live within their own paradigm, so no ego here. She is normal; it's us as parents who have a tough time catching up. Maybe you can address this topic in a letter for this time in her life, and another letter for when her children are teenagers– with sincerity and humor, of course.

Be mindful of her age when you discuss things she might be too young for. We all do that with children today. We think they have the capacity to process adult thoughts and ideas. They do not. She will certainly bring some of these topics to the discussion table – society is an open and sharing place – and not always with appropriate stuff. Be yourself when addressing these things. Let her know it worries you that she has so much available to her. Remain open to hear her and she will share more often. Finish by reminding her how wonderful she is and that she can do whatever she sets her mind to. Your voice will help teach her that she is important not only to you, but to the world. Make sure to label your envelopes well so she gets each letter at the right time, when she needs it.

About now, she may get her period. While it can be uncomfortable for a daughter to speak with her dad about this, *The Envelope System* gives you a powerful tool to help her. Does she already know the "Birds and the Bees?" Will you tell her? Will her mother? Will you do it together? Reading is often far less embarrassing than discussing things. Maybe you can purchase a book on puberty for her to open privately when the time comes. My father brought me flowers (no conversation - phew). Yes, it was embarrassing, but also wonderful. Set her up to see herself being treated well in her male-female relationships. My own daughter, however, wanted us both there for "the talk." Just in case, write a letter to cover it.

Yes, it's embarrassing to think about, but your understanding of her body development, hormone changes, emotions, and ability to support her with your knowledge and acceptance is powerful and has been shown to reduce symptoms of cramping and other reproductive issues. (Your positive influence is SO very important!)

It might only be two years of her life, but the Tween Years are important years where she continues to build confidence and self-image.

Starting Middle School

Dear Daddy,

I'm starting middle school today. The school is huge and I'm afraid of getting lost. Mom took me to walk around the halls and help me get my locker set up. I will forget my locker combination. Do you have any ideas on how I can remember it? Some Boy Scout trick?

I wish you were here with me.

Love you,

-xo

What do you want your daughter to know? Why do you want her to know it? Connecting with your purpose will help you achieve your goal. Be the best dad you can be.

Sample Tween Envelope

If you decide to write about the Birds and the Bees or when she gets her period, you really have to make that known on the outer envelope – as uncomfortable as it might seem. Just imagine how uncomfortable she will be if this is the Surprise Topic about which you chose to write. She needs to know what is inside the envelope so she can decide when to open it and hear your words.

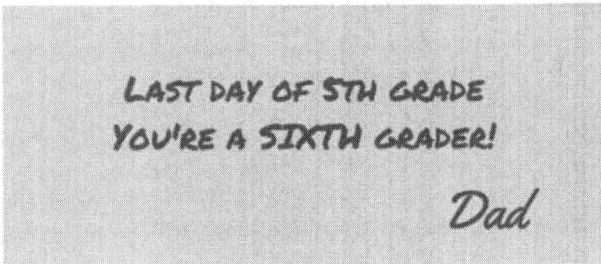

LAST DAY OF 5TH GRADE
YOU'RE A SIXTH GRADER!

Dad

Letter Ideas

TWEEN

Remember to include who, what, where, why, when, and how in your letters!

I'm So Proud Of You

Faith And Family

I Love You

You Are So Special To Me

You Are My Pretty Princess

What You Should Know About Boys

Peer Pressure

Importance Of Your Reputation

Respecting Yourself And Others

My First Crush

What I Loved About Middle School (include what middle school you went to)

What I Didn't Love About Middle School

Where I Lived In Middle School (include the address so she can visit someday)

Who My Friends Were (Are any still in your life?)

Funny Things People Did Back Then

Did You Take The Bus, Walk? How Did You Get To School?

What Activities I Participated In

What I Wish I'd Participated In

I Believe In…

I Am Most Grateful For….

What Is It That Really Matters?

Did I Do Well In School? What Were My Priorities?

What Was Considered Really Bad When I Was A Kid?

Where I Used To Hang Out After School

Words Of Wisdom

7

Teenager - 13 to 19 Years Old

First heartbreak (8th Grade)

Dear Daddy,

I can tell you this because you won't make fun of me. He likes her instead of me. He won't even talk to me. I don't understand what's wrong with me. Is there something wrong with me? What should I do? You're a guy. Why doesn't he like me? What do I need to do to make him like me?

-xo

For those of you who are *imagining* your daughter at this age, it might help to look around and take note of other girls at this age. It would be perfectly natural for her to be a bit boy-crazy, so what does she need to know about that? Maybe you have friends with teen-age daughters. Ask them what they are going through to help you be present with what your daughter may need from you at this age. Also, be attentive when you are out and you will notice this age group around every corner. Tune in to how they interact with each other. With boys. With adults. What are they wearing? What do you have to say about that? What hopes, feelings, concerns, thoughts come to mind about your little girl? Regardless of her age, she will always be your little girl.

In our focus groups, high school girls still want connection with their dads but they are becoming more independent and realize that they will be on their own or in college soon. Your girl wants to know what you think about her (always the good). Remember that your children hear constructive criticism as plain old criticism and judgment. Be specific about what she does well. Talk about that.

If you are trying to help her by pointing out the things she could improve, DON'T. She could take the negative words as being the truth about her and live her life subconsciously proving those negative words are who she *REALLY* is.

Now she is more ready to figure things out. What's working? What is not working? Why? This is your chance to help her understand how habits and thoughts are formed, and encourage her to be her own person. This includes deciding what she believes about life, and how to live and making her own path.

Consider this.

Why do you make the choices you make? Why do you think a certain way, do certain things, or have habits that other people either do, or do not have? Are your thoughts, beliefs, and habits getting you where you want to go? She is beginning to wondering about the same thing as this age and, even more so, into her twenties and beyond.

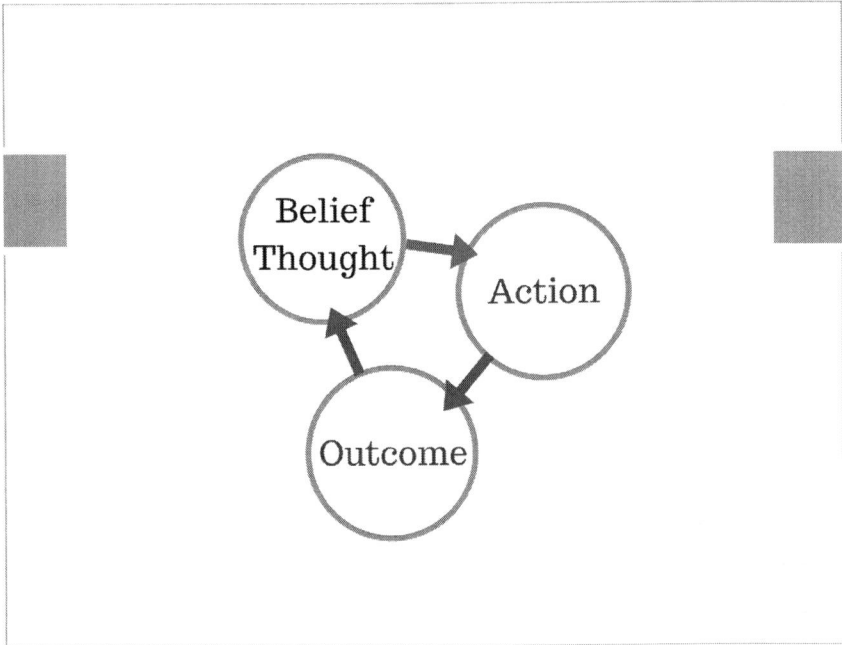

BELIEFS create ACTIONS. Does what you believe make you do things in a certain way? Yes, of course. If anyone challenges what you know to be true, you might not believe it. Why? Because that's what you think. But don't believe everything you think.

ACTIONS create OUTCOMES. If you believe, for example, that you are not good enough to succeed, every time you near success you will do something or procrastinate or, worse, you will not even try. What did you miss in your life that you want her to , "GO FOR (IT)?" When you LEAD her in a positive direction, she may follow.

Your OUTCOMES CONFIRM YOUR BELIEFS. When you procrastinate or do something to limit your success, it confirms your belief that you are not good enough, that you can't achieve success. Is it true? NO. But unless you think about it, decide what you want your outcome to be, and change your belief and actions to align with that result, it's probably not going to happen in the way you desire. And the cycle continues.

Be a positive source of who she is and describe her in the very best light. Write funny and positive things if you can but relax and be yourself. She still wants to know that her dad is proud of her and loves her. In many ways, she still, deep down inside, wants to be Daddy's Little Girl, but you also want her to be strong, kind, and make good decisions.

She still wants to hear "I Love You," "I'm Proud Of You," "You can do this!" and "You're Perfect Just The Way You Are." Write it.

BIG TIP: There are BOYS in her life! Take a very deep breath, dad! Boys can be a dreaded subject for any father but I urge you to become comfortable discussing this topic with her. Ever since her tween years, it is likely that boys have been a HUGE topic. She needs your input. Talking about the boys in her life can give her a great source of power and direction and you want her to choose a good partner, and a great husband. It's OK if this subject scares you, but it is your responsibility to guide your daughter. You were a young man once, so you know what boys are thinking and how they may let their hormones make decisions that will not serve your daughter well. In that respect, not much has changed except this is a scarier time because our children know a heck of a lot more than we did about sex when we were younger. However, they still really are not able to connect the dots with the reality of sex. What is safe? What is not OK? There are tons of resources out there to help guide you with this. A simple internet search will point you in a million directions, so search your own heart for what is truly best for your daughter. Share why you want that goodness for her. Asking people with kids this age also will help.

Some boys will betray her trust and use her dreamy thoughts of love as a way to interact with her sexually. You know not all boys are like this, but some are. How can she know the difference? What should she expect out of a relationship? What is special, sacred and what can she strive for? Make sure you consider that girls connect emotionally in all relationships. If you think it's OK for her to engage sexually with many men before she chooses "the one," then you are setting her up for failure. It's kind of like each boy she falls in love with gets a piece of her heart – so, what's left of her heart for the love of her life? Not much. Worse, she could become hardened and miss the best, most loving life because she is jaded. Think about what's best for her, not what you were horny for as a kid.

Remember that you and your relationships are her most influential teacher. Do you want that for her or something more? Some girls learn that a great way to become popular is to date many boys. Is that going to serve her well in the long run, or leave her with baggage no one wants? How do you feel about that for her?

Can your faith or spirituality lead her in this area? If she knows where you stand and that you care for her safety, she will consciously be able to set a goal for the issue and is far less likely to follow other people's ideals. She will have the tools (your wisdom and ideas as well as the freedom of intelligence she develops with your loving support) to be capable on her own.

If you think she should know about this from a trusted source, then write about it and offer the names of other people whom she can talk with that you know will support your ideals in a constructive, nonjudgmental way (talk with them first to be sure). You already know that having sexual relations increases the chance of sexually transmitted diseases but it's far deeper than that on an emotional level. Early sexual experiences can make sex something to pass the time rather than be an intimate and beautiful expression of a committed relationship. Protect her from becoming jaded, pregnant, or losing her ability to have loving and nurturing relationships by sharing your thoughts and ideals for her life.

First Boyfriend

Dad,

He asked me out today! I know he is a couple of years older, like a Junior, but he really likes me! He thinks I'm pretty and likes to talk with me. He's teaching me about cars and may even show me how to change my oil.

I hate not knowing how to do those things. I wish you were here to show me how. Mom always has to ask someone to help around the house. I think it bothers her because you used to do those things. No one is around to show me how to do those things either. All my friends are going hunting and working in the shop with their fathers. I wish we could do those things. If you were here...

I miss you so much.

I hope you are proud of me.

-xo

IMPORTANT: Your daughter is a girl. She wants to know she is pretty (and EVERY girl is pretty!) She loves romance, and loves love. She has no idea what the boys are thinking (be gentle). Some girls believe that because a boy pays attention to her, he loves her and they will live happily ever after. We want to believe our daughters are smarter than that but it's not her level of intelligence that affects her thinking. She is young and inexperienced and full of hormones and emotions; she is learning to cope. The truth is that she wants the fairy tale to be real at this stage. Your voice is very important in guiding her through reality without smashing her dreams, or distancing yourself from her by being too blunt. Write a letter about your hopes and dreams. She will hear you.

Sample Teenage Envelope

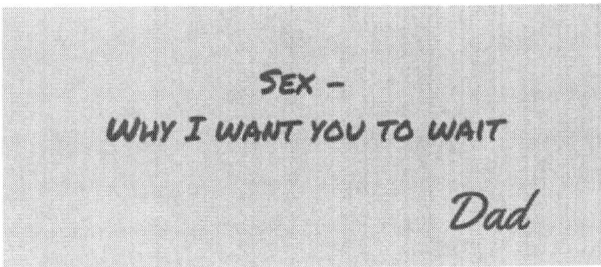

Yes, this needs to be discussed as early as possible. Kids are engaging in sexual relations in middle school these days! If you are not clear with your wishes and why, she will not put two and two together, so be clear.

Letter Ideas

TEENAGER

AGAIN, REMEMBER to include who, what, where, why, when, and how.

First Day Of Your Freshman Year

First Day Of Your Sophomore Year

First Day Of Your Junior Year

First Day Of Your Senior Year

To My High School Graduate

Importance Of Your Reputation

Respecting Yourself And Others

My High School Crush

What I Loved About High School (include what high school you attended)

What I Didn't Love About High School

Where I Lived In High School (include the address so she can visit someday)

Who My Friends Were (Are any still around?)

Funny Things People Did Back Then

Did You Take The Bus? Walk? How Did You Get To School?

What Activities I Participated In

What I Wish I'd Participated In

Did I Do Well In School? What Were My Priorities

What Was Considered Really Bad When I Was A Kid?

Where I Used To Hang Out After School

Faith And Family

Crazy Things I Did In High School (these are not meant to be ideas for her)

I Am Proud Of You

I Love You

You Are So Special To Me

Peer Pressure/Social Pressure

Partying – I Might Surprise You!

Anger - How To Handle It

When A Friend Betrays You – How To Get Through It

Sex – I Know This Is Embarrassing, But We Have To Talk About It

What Will You Do After High School?

All About My Favorite High School Teacher

Things I Learned In High School

What You Probably Don't Know About High School

What You Probably Don't Know About Life After High School

Friendships Now – Friendships Later

The Teacher I Liked Least And Why

Boys – Flirting, Dating And Some Dad Advice

My First Girlfriend/My First Kiss

My First Job, Jobs I Held in High School

8

AFTER HIGH SCHOOL

College, University, or Work (Ages 18-24)

In our focus groups, girls of every age want connection with their dad. The connection changes as girls age and become more self-reliant, but your daughter will always want to be supported and loved. She wants to know that (you think) she is capable, that she has everything she needs to be successful, and what you think about her (as long as what you think is good).

This is a larger chapter because, by now, your daughter realizes you are wise and useful, and her life has become bigger. She may be under the misunderstanding that adults don't make mistakes and feel a huge, unnecessary pressure to know lessons from experiences she had not had yet. Indeed the mistakes may have larger consequences but there is not an adult in the history of the planet that never made a mistake, at least in the eyes of another. What can you say to help her make wise choices, and know that everything is going to be OK -- no matter what? Step one foot in front of the other and keep working toward your goals.

Remember, girls of any age may hear constructive criticism (especially from their parents) as plain old criticism and judgment about her. She will take the negative words as being the truth about her and live her life subconsciously proving those negative words are who she *REALLY* is.

Your daughter is wonderful, marvelous, and awe-inspiring.

Remember that BELIEFS create ACTIONS that create RESULTS.

This is true of everything we think; it can be a cycle of failure but it can also be the cycle of success. Consider this cycle in your own life and use your experience to talk with her about things that really matter. This is a good time to look at why things are the way they are. Also, many men are good at finding one focus and working diligently on that, so focus on the very best for her and write your letters with that intention.

Please be a positive source of whom she is and describe her in the best light by writing about your experiences to help her figure things out and plan for a successful life. She still wants to know that her dad is proud of her and loves her and, as her responsibilities mount, deep down inside she will always want to be Daddy's Little Girl, this gives her softness to become the very best version of herself.

As already mentioned, she still wants to hear "I Love You," "I'm Proud Of You," and "You're Perfect Just The Way You Are."

The topics will be different for each child, but this real letter will help you know what she's thinking and help to remind you of some things you might want to prepare her for or guide her toward.

Dad,

I'm heading off to college and going to the same school where you and mom met. I really don't want to go there but I feel like I have to. Mom isn't saying it, but she gets really upset whenever I talk about going somewhere else. I guess I'm stuck.

I'm sure I'll get a fine education and everyone knows me, but here's the thing: I'm not her. I look a lot like her so everyone seems to think I have her same talents in Math. I'm a music major. Math is not my thing.

I am living on campus for the first few years. Thank goodness that Mom insisted on that. I want to experience college and I'm tired of feeling like I can't be me. I want to figure out who I am and being at home is not working for me.

I'm worried about Mom, Dad. It's been ten years since you died and she's still alone. How do I help her and be the person I want to be?

I wish you were here. I really do. I think she'd be a lot happier and I would be, too.

-xo

Sample Envelope

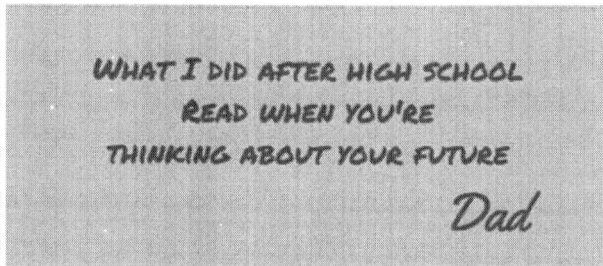

WHAT I DID AFTER HIGH SCHOOL
READ WHEN YOU'RE
THINKING ABOUT YOUR FUTURE

Dad

Letter Ideas

AFTER HIGH SCHOOL

REMEMBER to include who, what, where, why, when, and how.

What I Did After High School

Faith And Family

Why I Went to College (my school and choice of degree)

Did I Use My College Degree? If yes, is it how I expected?

I Wonder If You'll Go To College/University Or Will You Work?

What My Dating and Love Life Was Like

How I Met Your Mother

What Scared Me Moving Into Adulthood

How To Look At Things That Scare Us As An Opportunity To Be Excited About Doing Something New.

What Excited Me Moving Into Adulthood

What My Friends And I Did For Fun

How I See You At This Age

All About My First "Real" Job And How I Got It

How College/University/Working Changed Me

What I Thought I'd Do After High School And What I Actually Did

Importance Of Your Reputation

Respecting Yourself And Others

My First Place (include address so she can visit someday)

Who My Friends Were (Are any still around?)

Funny Things People Did Back Then

What Activities or Sports I Participated In

What I Wish I'd Participated In

I Am Proud Of You

I Love You

You Are So Special To Me

Partying – I Might Surprise You!

How You Handle Anger

What Happens When A Friend Betrays You

Sex – It Is A Three Letter Word, With A Lifetime Of Memories

Words Of Wisdom

You Can't Plan For Everything, But You Can Be Prepared for Anything – This Is How

ADULT LIFE

> *"IF YOU PLAN ON BEING ANYTHING*
> *LESS THAN YOU ARE CAPABLE OF*
> *BEING,*
> *YOU WILL PROBABLY BE UNHAPPY*
> *ALL THE DAYS OF YOUR LIFE."*
> *-ABRAHAM MASLOW*

Again, depending on the current age of your daughter, this might be a very difficult stage for you to write to her about. Remember that as time moves forward for her, you are becoming more of a confidant and your advice will be sought after – it will. You have laid all the groundwork throughout her childhood. This time she will be asking because she is listening and hearing your words. It is a pretty sure bet she will follow them, too. Through your loving interaction, she trusts your opinion. If this is not where you are at the moment, begin here. Relationships develop where you put your time and attention. Your gentle letters about your life and where you have triumphed and tried again will be an important part of this for you.

Look around at other young women of this age. You will start to see them at every turn. They are the recent college graduates, bright-eyed and eagerly stepping into the work force. They include the young mom you see at the store, at the park, and the young women at the movies. What do you hope for your daughter? How do you see her life? Maybe you see it more than one way. It's fine to write about many different choices. You don't know which one she will make into her reality. It doesn't matter. You're here to help no matter what unfolds in her life.

Relationship Crisis

Dad,

He almost hit me. I can't believe it. I stepped in instead of backing away, which is, I think, the only reason he didn't hit me. He was so mad at me, just for looking at his cell phone while we were at the pool hall. I wasn't snooping, just playing since I don't have one.

I think he's hiding something. What should I do? Break up with him? Give him another chance? I think I'm just going to ride this out and see what happens.

-xo

According to The Facts: **Violence Against Women & Millennium Development Goals** (compiled by UNIFEM, 2010), up to 76 percent of women are targeted for physical and/or sexual violence in their lifetime. Most of this violence takes place within intimate relationships, with many women (ranging from 9 percent to 70 percent) reporting their husbands or partners as the perpetrator.

If this were your daughter, what would you say to her? Most of us have cell phones now, but it's the overall tune of this letter that begs for a fatherly response.

Sample Envelope for Adult Life

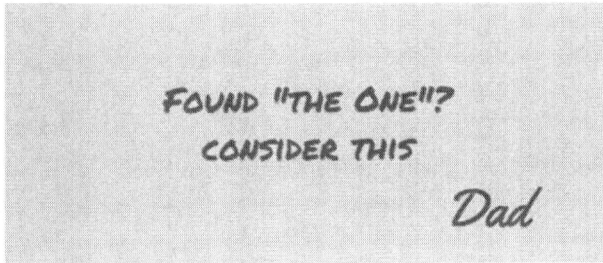

FOUND "THE ONE"?
CONSIDER THIS

Dad

BIG TIP:

Something to think about regarding friendship

What have friendships meant in your life? When have people stepped up to help you? When have you had the chance to help someone else? Do you have funny memories to share, or something you learned?

Write whatever you think she should hear about friendships.

And then, there is LOVE....

LOVE

Before she finds the love of her life, there will be boys who come and go. There is that rare couple who meets early in life and knows it is meant to be. These relationships are so precious and it is what every girl wants! In today's society though, that is the rare *Love Story*. If you want to see your daughter having one of these, go ahead! Visualize it and share your thoughts and feelings. How awesome to let her know that you believe this is possible for her!

Mostly though, I am guessing that when a dad thinks about his daughter and love, he has a few concerns that are more serious.

Sex is great and necessary in a marriage, but if you don't want your girl to be having sex at a young age, tell her in a loving way. Share your experience. If you waited and are glad, tell her. If you didn't wait and can see the benefits of waiting, share that. She will not be told what to do, but if you share your thoughts, chances are she will listen. Use examples such as friends' experiences and your observations of where certain decisions can lead. Remind her that she is an equal partner in a relationship and she must think about what she really wants. Many couples marry without discussing what each hopes for the future and this can create a lot of discord. If she wants a husband who can be there for the family, then she should focus on choosing a man who openly agrees and feels the same way.

Again, what do you want for her life? Peace? Happiness? Good relationships? Knowing that she is special? Should she be the only one in her partner's life? How can you encourage her to be capable and independent? A good partner and friend? Please tell her she can be all of these things, and remind her that mistakes are only ways to build on ourselves and possibly decide what we really want. Either you'll have to keep on trying to get it right, or you'll learn something about life and move on.

We learn as we get older that attitude is everything and those of us who live with the understanding that there are truly no mistakes in life have a far different outcome than those who believe they are a victim and being picked on. I hope that as you look back with your eyes and heart are wide open to share with her the great learning opportunities that come out of even the worst circumstances. Sometimes your best learning has come from the way you moved forward from things not going as planned. Let her know glitches are just a part of life. Help her discover how to process mistakes, evaluate them, and let them go to she can move on in the most positive way possible.

With whom do you want her to be? What are the qualities of a good partner? What personal qualities would you be proud to welcome into your family and have parent your grandchildren? Who is this person that will take loving care of your daughter (hopefully by creating a mutually caring relationship) for the rest of her days?

Think about that and let her know. This is of utmost importance. She will seek a partner who has elements of you. Writing these letters is a great way to ensure that she chooses from a place of power, not circumstance.

Which brings us to … what are your best qualities? Describe your best self and mention the things you're proud of or happy about in your relationships.

She may not marry her first love, although wouldn't that be nice. It is more likely that she will fall in love and, without much thought, decide that this is the man with whom she wants to spend forever. That might be how you did it, but perhaps there is a better way. Classes are available to couples before they marry, but they usually go as a prerequisite to getting married in a particular church AFTER the decisions have already been made. When she gets engaged, the chances of her cancelling the big day are close to nil. Even if she begins to realize this is perhaps not her best match, she will marry him anyway, hoping he will change.

People only change if they want to and marriage can actually solidify poor habits. A girl cannot change any boy, or vice versa. People must want to change for themselves and, indeed, each family has a variety of ways of doing things that will be different than the way your family does it. It's not necessarily bad, but your girl must know what she feels most strongly about in order to assess whether it's a deal breaker or to relax about it. Let her know about that while maintaining a mature outlook on the negative experiences that may have happened in your life with in-laws and such.

IMPORTANT: If she is thinking about making a commitment, you may want to come up with questions she must have the answers to before they ever even seriously talk about becoming engaged.

Questions could include: What is your opinion about the role of a wife? What is the role of a husband? Who does what chores? Who cooks? Who will take off work if a child needs to be home? What are the responsibilities of a man? Of a woman? Should kids do chores? Will they take them to church? What religion? What about health-care choices, dishes, groceries? Do they think they have to work long hours to make the amount of money to live the life they desire or will they live doing what they love and money is not that important? What are their views on money, kids, work, places to live, hobbies they share, if any. Who pays the bills, makes investments, researches how to invest? If their opinions differ they may cause conflict unless they are resolved consciously with conversation. Make a checklist for them to work from. How cool would that be?

Also, consider that she may not choose to do things in the same way that you do, nor may she live a conventional life. You would never want to assume her thoughts or preferences, but I want to encourage you to support her with positive praise and love in any and all circumstances.

The list of things to write about is endless but unless she sits down with her intended partner for life and discusses all these life decisions, she is guessing and that may not provide her with the best outcome. What is your experience? What do you wish you'd thought about? Long before we commit to a relationship, all of these topics are decided in our minds due to our upbringing, but we never quite understand that the person in the relationship with us could have a completely different set of unspoken rules.

Encourage her to be strong and discuss this with her intended partner.

Sample Envelope – Love

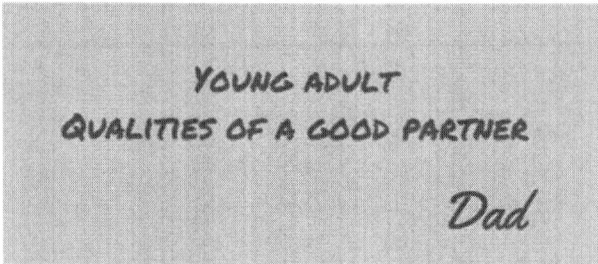

YOUNG ADULT
QUALITIES OF A GOOD PARTNER

Dad

Letter Ideas

LOVE

Use all of the ideas mentioned in the previous pages. Here are some others that are appropriate now and moving forward in her life.

Faith And Beliefs, Where She Can Draw Strength And Support

Budgeting

Healthy Habits I Wish I'd Followed

Planning

Goals

Buying Your First Home

Friendships

Peer Pressure

Teaching People

How You Should Be Treated By Others

How I Met Your Mom

What Was My Most Embarrassing Dating Moment?

Relationships And Sex – Keeping It Healthy

I'm So Proud Of You, I Love You, You Are So Special,

You Deserve: _____

I Believe In…

Is It Normal For A Guy To Hibernate In His Man Cave For Hours Watching Television?

TIP: YES, it is! Men tend to prefer one thing at a time and are conscious about their need to process and relax for a moment sometimes. Women are constantly "on" and if another woman is quiet, it alerts her that something could be wrong. Because girls are gatherers, she tries to talk about it to gather information. This is why women ask if everything is OK when you are quiet (unless she has learned that it's OK for a man to be quiet sometimes). Men and women think differently and are alerted differently when something is wrong. Be kind and let he know about this.

How To Say No If Someone Wants Something You Do Not

What I Want For You In Your Love Relationship(s)

Communication And Love

Listen To Your Little Voice – It Keeps You Safe. LISTEN

Selecting A Spouse --- What To Look For, Values, Experiences, Family Experience

Faith And Spirituality

Words Of Wisdom

What Men Think About Sex.

TIP: Men are visual, and may not, at first, long for life-long love and stability in their partner. Is that just something she has to live with (NO) or can she make joint, consensual decisions about when to share her body? (YES) I know there is a lot of talk of sex and other difficult topics, but this is the facts of life, and where your daughter really needs your input and guidance.

Dating 101

I Am Most Grateful For....

Things That Really Matter

9

Engagement And Her Wedding

Engagement

If you're ill, this may be one of the most difficult topics for you to write about – or even to think about. While I know NONE of this is easy to do, you must press on. This is one of those special times both father and daughter dream about in nearly the same way but I want to remind you about the life and passing of Adrian, so that you are prepared in case the unthinkable happens. As you held your baby girl just after she was born, you probably thought about walking her down the aisle. What if your little girl's wedding day happens without you?

You're OK. This is for her; you can do it.

If you need counseling or conversations with her mother to understand more fully what your daughter will be going through at this time, make sure you seek it. Your daughter is not the only one who risks losing you and, even if you and your daughter's mother don't get along, chances are your ex will understand your desire to connect with your daughter on this matter and is willing to help you. And, while this will be sentimental and may be heart wrenching for her, too, you want your messages to be heartfelt and as positive as possible. She is going to feel your absence. Speak to that and find the strength and the courage to find a way to be there in your daughter's life at this special time.

IMPORTANT: Probably the most important thing to convey to your daughter is that she must tell her husband what she wants, thinks, needs, likes etc., and with as little emotion as possible. Men are intelligent, but not mind readers no matter how many hints we drop or how obvious we think something is. Men are not women. Tell her to tell him straight out and he will respect that.

So, yes! Your daughter is engaged! Imagine her at this age. She is excited and hopeful for the future. She wants to know that she will be a great wife and, perhaps, mother someday. She is older now, but she still needs advice and encouragement as she prepares for her marriage, and just as much from her dad as from her mom. This often surprises men.

Many of the things you have written to her about dating overlap with considerations about marriage. Marriage is like any adventure, and she and her partner need to prepare in order to really succeed. Are you excited for her? What are your hopes and dreams for her and her husband? Would you like the young man to ask you for her hand in marriage? What criteria would determine a blessing, or a "hit the road?" What would you like the celebration to look like? A list of "musts" will guide you all in the right direction, regardless of how long you have together. Remember our children learn more from what we do than from what we say, so if you are not like the man on your list, start to change now or she may not choose the type of man you describe.

Do you wish you'd asked your partner a few questions before you married? Are there things you wished you'd known? How do you encourage your daughter to be sure this is "the one," and how do you encourage her about all that takes place in the commitment of marriage?

What does a young woman need to know about marriage? What were the struggles you felt in your own marriage, or relationships? How could your experience help her? What can she be conscious of and plan for to keep her love alive? What does her new partner need from her? What did you need and receive and what did you need and compromise on? What do you look back on and wish you'd really pursued? Relationships normally have high points and low points. Let her know that's perfectly normal. As the saying goes, attitude is everything, so choose a good one.

In our focus groups, young ladies still want to hear funny things from their dad but they are now looking at having their own family. Your daughter wants to know about communication with her partner-to-be, how to deal with being new parents, in-laws, what is or what could be her role in their relationship.

As parents, we all hope our children will discuss these important things with their potential life-partner before marriage so they are on the same page and will live as well as possible with that person, but we know from experience that's probably not the case. When we are in love, we all see the person we are with as perfect. No one is perfect; don't expect that, and question it if it is because there should be a healthy give and take in a relationship. It is not one-sided.

To make matters worse, it would seem that if they are in a sexual relationship, the very thing that constantly revives the bliss and joy of a marriage by somewhat dulling us toward our partner's faults (lovemaking) also makes our sexually active children think their partner can do no wrong. Regardless of your experience, this is unchartered waters for her and she needs your ideas and experience to help her make her decisions.

Yes, today our kids are much more confident about these things and they think they have it all under control. We hear a lot of "don't worry; it is all good!" The reality is that there has to be a way to share with them, to ensure they have as many tools as possible to keep it "all good."

Your gift of letters is a subtle and effective way to accomplish this.

WHAT is the SECRET to a long, successful partnership? What have you learned from your marriage or separation?

If her experience from your relationships is that marriages fail, she should know why and what you learned. Help her. If she has a nurturing, long-lasting parental relationship, then she will seek your input on how to navigate the struggles and the compromise of marriage. Remind her that relationships are about two people, and rarely do two people always agree, and that's OK. No two people approach marriage in the same way. You are envisioning her engagement and marriage – and doing what you need to in providing wisdom for all things that come along – good and bad.

She still wants to hear "I Love You," "I'm Proud Of You," and "You're Perfect Just The Way You Are." This is always a great place to start, no matter what age you are writing for.

Remember to just be honest and kind. Be positive about what you want to say about her; be positive in your wording and praise her with what she did right... Include who, what, where, why, when and how.

Sample Envelope – Engagement

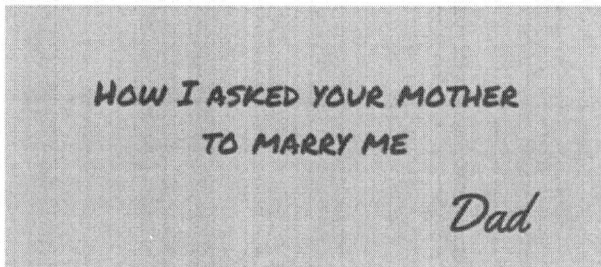

LETTER IDEAS

Engagement

How I Asked Your Mother To Marry Me. My Version

How I Asked Your Mother To Marry Me. Her Version

Is It Important To Me That He Asks For Your Hand? Why?

Did I Ask For Your Mom's Hand In Marriage? Why or Why Not?

Things I Thought About Before Getting Married

What Is Love, Really?

What I Thought I Knew, But Changed My Mind

Will Marriage Be Easy If We Are Meant To Be Together?

Will We Only Fight If We Were Not Meant To Be?

How To Resolve Arguments

Compromise Is The Food Of Life, But It Must Be Enjoyed By All

What If You Change Your Mind?

Is Marriage Important To Me

What I Think About Living Together, And Why

What Commitment Means

Hard Times In Marriage - What You Should Know.

How Do You Know He Is The One?

The Man I See Asking You To Marry Him

Faith And Spirituality

How I See You And Your Mom Making Wedding Plans

What I Would Say If I Was In The Room With You

I Believe In...

I Am Most Grateful For....

What Is It That Really Matters?

I Hope You Include A Special Place For Me

The Conversation I Would Have With Your Fiancé

How Many Children Does He Want?

Responsibilities With Children, Finances, Working ... And Lots Of Other Good Questions You MUST Discuss With Your Partner Before Getting Engaged or Tying The Knot

Words of Wisdom

Her Wedding

She is A BRIDE! WOW!

What is important to you in regards to her wedding? Do you love a certain song? Do you have a favorite prayer or any other wedding tradition that is important to you? Are you hoping to walk her down the aisle? Why? How do you anticipate feeling at that moment? Will you cry? Can you admit to her that you will be overcome with emotions? Father-daughter relationships can be tough, but whether you are close at the moment or not, daddies always have a soft spot for their little girls. She will love to know about how you will feel in that moment of her upcoming wedding.

Maybe you want to write a toast. What do you hope to share? There are so many ideas – maybe the best suggestion is to have a fun conversation with your daughter about her dream wedding. Children are not only resilient, they are naturally intuitive and all knowing. You might get a huge surprise in having that conversation with her, even at whatever age she is right now.

If you choose to do this, you really have to write a letter about that entire conversation for her to read later.

If you want her to enjoy a keepsake, or a special heirloom piece, include this information in the envelope. Or if a more valuable piece is being kept for her, let her know where she can find it.

Consider purchasing a bracelet or other piece of jewelry, wrap it for her and be sure to include a letter about why you chose that particular piece, how you felt when you found the piece, and how it made you feel about her getting married. If it's an heirloom piece of jewelry, let her know who owned the jewelry. Anything you write about it is helpful so she knows as much as you do about the piece. Include a prayer or thought with the jewelry.

If you are not with her to share this envelope, then there is nothing you can do to shield her from the pain of losing you.

What you CAN DO, however, is continue to bond with her with the strong emotions she will be feeling at this important time of her life.

In this way, if she can't be on your arm, you can be on hers.

Getting Married

Well Daddy, today is the big day! I'm getting married. Grandpa is walking me down the aisle. I wish it was you but he will do a great job. He's also doing the ceremony. I have a blue candle burning for you. I remember it's your favorite color. Mine, too. No coincidence there.

Craig is great. Mom loves him! I haven't seen her this happy in years. Send me a rainbow, OK?

Love you and miss you!

-xo

(There was a double rainbow at our reception that night.)

Sample Envelope - Her Wedding

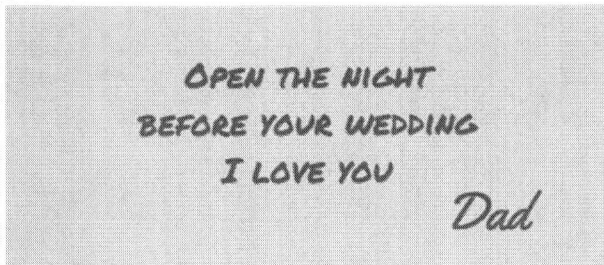

OPEN THE NIGHT
BEFORE YOUR WEDDING
I LOVE YOU
Dad

LETTER IDEAS

Her Wedding

What Is Important To Me At Your Wedding?

The Value Of Sex In Marriage

Why Never Saying The D-Word Is Important (Saying "divorce" damages the relationship by hurting each other and breeding mistrust.)

My Favorite Wedding Songs

Faith And Spirituality

My Favorite Part Of Weddings

Song For Our Father-Daughter Dance And Why

What I Want To Say To You During Our Father-Daughter Dance

To My Daughter, You're A Bride

I'm So Proud Of You – I Love You

You Are So Special To Me

My Favorite Prayer

Other Wedding Things That Are Important To Me

Why You Will Always Be "Daddy's Little Girl"

How Boys And Girls Still Think Differently As Adults

How I Feel Seeing You At The Alter

Funny Stories From Your Wedding Celebration

Decide That You Are In A Lifelong Relationship. All Relationships Have Ups And Downs, Focus On Working It Out.

Mentors (find others who have the same ideas about love and marriage)

Reminder: Men Are Not Mind Readers. Do Not Hint, Do Not Assume He Should Know. Tell Him Clearly What You Think, Want, Need, See.

What To Do When You think There is No Hope In Your Relationship. Number 1: Are You Safe?

Funny Stories During Your Marriage

Words Of Wisdom

I Believe In…

I Am Most Grateful For….

What Really Matters?

Buying Your First Home

Insurance And Other Things To Know About

Making It Work When He Doesn't Do What You Thought He Would

The Differences Between Men And Women

Our own house

DAD! What the heck am I supposed to do! I have repairs that most normal girls know how to fix.

How, exactly, do I caulk the tub? For that matter, which caulk to do I buy? There are a million!

I really need help with some electrical work in the basement and the fan over the table needs replacing. Weren't you an electrician in the Navy? By the way, I have your table saw in my garage and can't find the guard ... did you happen to ever use it?

I'm feeling totally out of my depth here, Dad. Why couldn't you have been around to teach me all these things? I need you.

It's not your fault. Please don't take it that way. I just wish you were here. I miss you so much, nearly twenty-five years later.

-xo

10

PARENTING

Your child is a parent or will soon be one.

There is so much that you've learned and, maybe at this point in this project, you have learned even more. You are offering your daughter all the things you think are good, things you wish you'd never done, or things you wish you HAD done. She is connecting with you deeply and that will wrap around her for all of her days.

How miraculous that you can help her!

Perhaps through letters about your own experiences and thoughts about fatherhood, you can help her know what her partner is experiencing during her pregnancy, labor, and the appearance of their new baby. Be sure to support her by making sure she knows she is capable of making good decisions. Again, this life event may be difficult to imagine right now, but try. As you well know, parenting takes a lot of support to achieve the best results. Let her know that whatever her choice is, you admire her for living in the best way she knows.

If this stage is too difficult to imagine, please continue to write anyway. You are doing this so your daughter has what she needs from you forever. You can do this. Write about your thoughts and experiences … how you and her mother traveled this journey. Your fears; your hopes. Let her know how amazing parenting is.

What about childbirth? Were you terrified when your daughter was born? Were you even there when she was born? If not, why? What happened when she was born? Were you allowed in the room? Was she born at home? Did you hold her right away? She wants to know your perspective and whatever you can remember. Tell her she is going to be a great mother. Hearing your confidence will make her be a better mother. It's true. Girls need encouragement and support. Your words will give her the confidence to make tough decisions, be strong when she needs to be, and relax as much as possible. You know everything is going to be OK, but with a crying baby (your grandchild) in her arms, dinner unplanned, and her husband needing her, too, never mind that she just needs a break, she needs reassurance that this too shall pass, that everything will be OK. Tell her that.

How can she help her husband lead their family? What kinds of things might be happening in their life now that could be setting them up for trouble later? What things should they be sure to always do … Date Night, for example?

Her children are your grandchildren! This may be the farthest thing from your mind right now but it will probably happen and your daughter needs your advice. What does she need to know? Can you offer her a man's point of view? How did you manage it? What should she ask from her husband? Will it all work out? Think back and remember what it was like when she was a baby. What did you need? Go from there.

Do you have favorite names you'd like her to consider for her children, or that you think are funny? Is there a family tradition such as using the father's given name as a middle name for the baby? Are there any customs or traditions she can honor and enjoy?

What would you like to do with your grandkids? Would you like to take them for the weekend, or buy their winter clothing? How can you support her? What did you and her mother need (and perhaps didn't get) that you could provide for her now?

It's also possible that your daughter will get pregnant before she is married. If you're hoping she will wait until marriage, then write a letter about your hopes for her life, but be careful that you are kind and loving just in case she is an unwed mother. If she is in this situation, she will need your understanding and support. Think about these things and come up with supportive words that work for you.

In our focus groups, girls shared that if they could hear that their dad was proud of them, it would change their life.

Write whatever you think she should hear, from a position of pride and full-blown love for the person she has become. This type of kindness and support will make any situation move forward with more power and positivity, thereby reducing the frequency of the negative. We get what we focus on, so focus on what's good about every situation.

Sample Envelope – Parenting

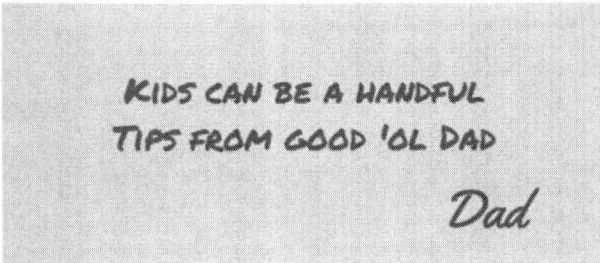

KIDS CAN BE A HANDFUL
TIPS FROM GOOD 'OL DAD

Dad

Letter Ideas

PARENTS

What do you want for your kids? Focus on that. What do you hope your children will instill in their children? Values, relationships, kindness, respect for nature and our environment? Chores, allowance, a positive relationship with money? How we did it, why, and would we do it that way again?

Remember you are writing as if this is happening because, for her, it is.

You Are A Mother, That's Weird Since Today You....

Faith And Spirituality

What Your Kids Really Need And What They Don't

How I Feel About Being A Grandparent

What Grandfather Name I Would Like To Be Called

My Plans With The Grandkids

I Bet I'll Have ___ Grandkids Because ...

When You Were Little You Used To Play, 'Mommy'

How To Keep Your Relationship Strong With Your Husband After Children

What I Wish I Knew About Babies, Children, Childbirth....

Schedule Date Nights! Do It, Here's Why!

Things My Parents Did For Us

What I Thought Of Your Mom's Body Through Pregnancy. (Only if you were in awe and thought it was great and she was beautiful.)

Things I Did To Help Out Until You Were Born

Things I Did To Help Out After You Were Born

Asking For Help – DO IT!

How We Prepared Your Bedroom

Words Of Wisdom

What Is Really Important

Have You Thought About Writing Letters To Your Baby? Start Writing Letters To Your Own Children Now!

How Your Grandparents Raised Me

11

YOUR MOTHER AND ME

We often model our relationships after what was modeled to us growing up. As much as we fight to NOT BE LIKE OUR PARENTS, we usually take on at least some of their traits because we learn more from what we see, and learn less from what we are told. Attitude is everything. Pick a good one.

Some of the questions for the Engagement and Marriage chapters are useful reminders here as well; feel free to flip back to those sections for more ideas.

50 percent Mom

+ 50 percent Dad

= 100 percent Child

Your daughter will want to know about your relationship with her mother. Whether it's good or bad, pull out the good. Your daughter is half your DNA and half her mother's DNA. You want her to be a positive 50 percent you plus a positive 50 percent her mother to equal 100 percent full and healthy woman.

Things you write from this section continue to help her feel secure in who she is. Knowing about your relationships will help her.

Sample Envelope - Your Mother and Me

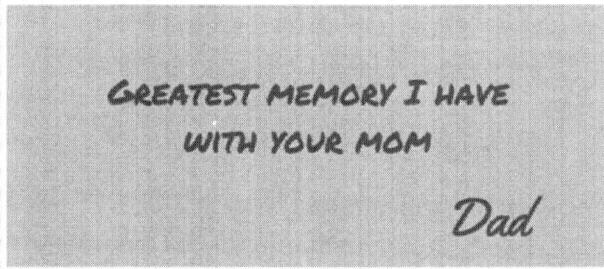

GREATEST MEMORY I HAVE
WITH YOUR MOM

Dad

Letter ideas

YOUR MOTHER AND ME

Favorite Date With Mom

A Great Memory I Have Of Your Mom

I Fell In Love With Your Mom Because …

What I Remember About Our Wedding

What I Did Right

What I Wish I'd Done

You Should Know What I Think About Your Mom (If you're in a tumultuous relationship, stick with the positive things. You were, after all, close enough to conceive a child.)

How I Met Your Mother, My Side

How I Met Your Mother, What She Will Say

How We Decided To Get Married, My Side

How We Decided To Get Married, What She Will Say

When I Married Your Mother: Our Wedding

Things I Remember About That Day

Something Stupid I Wish I Had Not Done

My Relationship With Your Mother

I'm So Proud Of You, I Love You, And You Are So Special To Me

My Greatest Regret

I Believe In...

What I Am Most Grateful For

What Is Really Important To Know About Us

What Will I Set Out To Achieve Or Change?

Our Bucket List

12

Between You AND Me

This section is for anything extra that might come to your mind to share with your daughter, perhaps things between the two of you that are special or need to be said. Maybe there is something she should know about another relationship that will bring her enlightenment or clarity.

Also, forgiveness is a beautiful thing and asking for forgiveness is going to be necessary at some point in her life. She will learn from you -- no matter what your actions -- so teach her that asking for forgiveness, being truthful, and planning for her life is achievable. Even if you aren't able to accomplish the things you wanted to, she can if you offer it as an option with your support and encouragement.

Change is normal and to be expected. How can you help her through the big stuff that trips us all up? Sometimes she needs to hear that everything is going to be OK.

My father has been gone from this life, since February of 2009. I was in my mid-forties when he died, but I was still single and had always had the assurance that there was a place to spend the holidays. However, with his passing, we would never again spend our holidays together in the home where our family had lived for my entire life.

When I think about things I wish my dad had told me, there are several: How did he meet my mom? Did he plan to marry her that day when they went with another couple to elope in Georgia (and my parents got married!)? What was it about being a Junior High principal that he disliked so much? What were the happiest times of his childhood? Why was he against going to church with the family? How was he different when he came home for World War II than before he went?

My dad had lost both his parents. How did that affect him?

Almost a year after my dad passed, I got engaged. It was hard to plan the wedding knowing that neither of my parents would be there. What would he have said to me on my wedding day? I was his baby girl and it was common knowledge that I was his favorite – how would he have felt that day, giving me away?

My parents were married for fifty-nine years and eleven months, so what advice could he have offered to help me create a successful marriage? What could he have told me about the importance of holidays and family traditions?

What advice could he have provided about money management in marriage? What would he say was the most important trait to look for in a husband? My husband has two children and I am now a stepmother. What parenting advice would he say is most important? What was the best/ worst parenting advice he ever received? What was his first thought the moment he saw me? What was one thing I did that made him proud? What were his dreams for me?

I have so many more questions. I miss him.

The answers to my questions will never come, but today you can make sure your child knows the answers. I'd love to know my dad like that.

-- Myra

Sample Envelope - Between You And Me

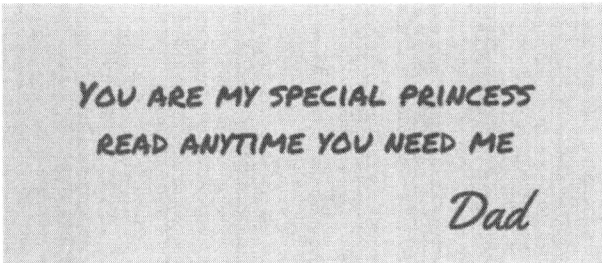

YOU ARE MY SPECIAL PRINCESS
READ ANYTIME YOU NEED ME

Dad

Letter ideas

JUST BETWEEN YOU AND ME

I'm So Proud Of You, I Love You, You Are So Special To Me

Things You Should Know

What I Want For You

You Are Smart Enough To Think For Yourself

Knowing How And When To Compromise

You Don't Have To Be Perfect

Growing Up I Felt:

I Remember…

What Do You See In Her That Is Part Of You, Or Like You

What Makes Her So Precious?

Sweet Memories Of You And Your Child

Things You Did Together Or For Each Other; Why You Like That

Things Your Daughter Used To Say

Basic Car Maintenance (Why Not?)

I Will Never Leave You

You Should Know What I Think About You

I Never Want To Leave You

Silliest Thing You Did

Silliest Thing I've Done So When You Do Something Stupid You Know You're Not Alone

Pep Talk To Look At When She Has Something Big Coming Up - You Can Do It!

My Moral Compass: Right From Wrong

Something Stupid I Wish I Had Not Done

Basic Choices: Good, Bad, Learned, You Don't Have To Be Perfect

When Faced With A Big Decision, Do You Go With Your Gut Or Your Heart?

In Times Of Joy, I Like To:

In Difficult Times, I Like To:

Sometimes Life Sucks, Now What?

What I Want You To Remember In Difficult Times

How To Have A Good Attitude About Money

What Can You Do For Fun, Or To Plan When You Don't Have Much Money

What Really Matters In Life

Something You Need To Know

Everyone Has A Purpose, Find Yours

Recurrent Dreams I Have Or Have Had

If You Can't Plan For Everything, How To Be Prepared For Anything

Believe In Yourself!

When To Compromise (it's OK)

How To Treat People

You Are Always My Princess

Some Things She Might Be Wondering About

Read the list and see if you think she might like to know the answers to some of these questions. Feel free to photocopy this page and simply write in the answers. If you enjoy being creative, photocopy the questions and cut each one out individually to glue onto the letter. Be descriptive; she wants all the details. Be specific and kind.

Are you glad you had me?

What do you like about me?

What do you think I can do when I grow up?

Do you think I'm special?

Do you love me?

What's the best thing about me?

What am I good at?

What are my strengths?

What can you see me doing when I grow up?

What do I look for when I'm buying a house?

How do you feel about me getting a tattoo?

Tell me a story about when you got drunk.

13

Life Happens

Yes, life happens and it's going to happen for your little girl. You have the chance here to prepare her for tough times and to help her know that she is never alone. What resources do you use, or what would you like her to use? Family, friends, faith, church, community programs, planning ... so much goes into living successfully and to digging ourselves out of the tough stuff.

What do you want to share with her?

First Major Breakup

Dad,

What am I going to do? Am I destined to be alone? We broke up tonight! He cheated on me while Mom and I were on vacation! I hate him! Can you come back, just for a day and beat him up for me? Please?

I can't believe he would do that to me!

-xo

How would you have her work through the jerks in her life? It might not be a relationship. It could be a co-worker or a friend.

You may not be that guy who's deeply connected to sharing feelings, or to your "feminine side," but knowing how a man works is helpful for a girl. It's OK if you say things like, "I'm not sure if all men think this way," because we all operate from our own belief system (that might be working or might not). It's OK. You have answers. She needs to have them before she really needs them, and receiving them via a nonjudgmental letter will increase your chances that she will actually read, absorb, and follow through with what you've learned the hard way.

She may not identify with your ways, but knowing how you deal with things will help her expand her thinking so she can better adapt to the different people she will encounter, even know what to expect from a man, and even her sons. Men and women, boys and girls all think and act differently.

If you are embarrassed by your behavior, or wish you'd done things differently, share that with her. But remember, we get what we focus on, so round your message out with something of strength, such as your observations and ideas for next time. Kids observe a lot. She just wants the real you. She will need to insert her own life experiences but knowing yours will help.

I Wish You Were Here

I went out to my father's grave today. It was a terrible day for me and I needed my father. I'd been out to his grave many times since getting my driver's license, but today was different. I was devastated and, for the first and last time, sat on the headstone. I needed a hug from my father like nothing else, and obviously, he wasn't able to be there. I sat at his grave and cried for hours.

"I wish you were here today. I really need you."

-xo

Lots of girls feel this way with their dad right in the next room. How can you be there, no matter what happens? Yes, keep writing letters. And give them to her.

ENVELOPE IDEAS when Life Happens

HIGH SCHOOL
WHEN THINGS AREN'T GOING RIGHT
AND YOU FEEL ALONE
Dad

Letter ideas

WHEN LIFE HAPPENS

Believe In Yourself

Silliest Thing I've Done So When You Do Something Stupid, You Know You're Not Alone

I Got Fired/Lost My Job (When One Door Closes Another Opens)

Pep Talk That You Can Look At When You Have A Big Thing Coming Up - You Can Do It! You Don't Have To Be Perfect

My Moral Compass -- Right From Wrong

Something Stupid I Wish I Had Not Done

Basic Choices: Good, Bad, Learned, Don't Have To Be Perfect

When Faced With A Big Decision, Do You Go With Your Gut Or Your Heart?

In Times Of Joy, I Like To:

In Difficult Times, I Like To:

Sometimes Life Sucks, Now What?

What I Want You To Remember In Difficult Times

I'm So Proud Of You, I Love You, and You Are So Special To Me

How To Have A Good Attitude About Money

Lack Of Money

I Believe In You

I Am Most Grateful For....

What Is It That Really Matters?

14

All About Me

You have already shared so much with your daughter, and now you get to share things about you. While you have revealed a lot in this process, this is the part where it becomes all about you – your likes, your dislikes, and whatever it might be that you have not written about yet.

Your daughter will have what others don't: a letter to read about all of your favorite things!

Sample All About Me Envelope

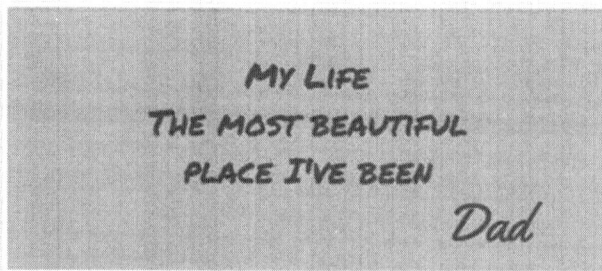

Letter ideas

ALL ABOUT ME

My First Kiss. Who? When? Did I Kiss Her Again?

If I Could Pick A Part Of The Country I Could Live In But Didn't, Where Is It?

I Want To Be Your (Hero?): _____

How I Feel About Myself (I Don't Want To Tell You And Why)

If I Had It To Do Over, Where Would I Live? Where Would I Go To Start My Life?

Ginger Or Mary Ann? (Who Would You Choose If Left On A Deserted Island? You may need to explain *Gilligan's Island* if your child has never watched it.)

Special Times

Special Feelings

Special Words

When Was I The Happiest

When Was I The Saddest

My Favorite Time: AM or PM

My Favorite Memory

My Favorite People

My Favorite Hobby

My Favorite: Quiet Time? Loud Time?

My Favorite Time Of My Life

Friendships

My Favorite Tie

My Favorite Thing About You

I Believe In...

What I Took For Granted

People I Missed Along The Way

Something I Could Never Get Myself To Do, And Wanted To

I Am Most Grateful For....

What Did I Think Really Matters? What Actually Does?

15

Your Legacy

A VERY PERSONAL CHOICE
ONLY YOU CAN MAKE

It is true that you will leave people behind who will miss you, and they will make decisions about how to honor your memory. Because you have the gift of time, today you can begin to prepare your family to live full and vibrant lives after they have mourned your passing.

Whether they move on in peace or with anger, regret and fear may largely depend on how you leave your relationships. Consider what you want for your loved ones. In the event of your passing, you will want to be remembered, but I hope that you don't want your family never to love again or to be alone forever in your honor. Give the gift of LIFE to those you leave behind by telling them that it's OK to keep living, and that that's what you WANT them to do.

A friend of mine, Bruce, has a terrific story to share about love, loss, and continued living after his wife, Terrilynn, died several years ago.

Terrilynn knew she was dying, so she left her husband, children, and family a wonderful gift – the gift of a life filled with love and opportunity after her death. Let me explain.

Before she passed, Terrilynn made scrapbooks and shared her life with her children with journal entries and notes. She also thought about how to release her husband from feeling as if he had to serve her memory for the rest of his life.

You may or may not have the will to scrapbook, but what I hope you hear is the release she gave Bruce. She told him that she was praying for a new wife for him and a loving mother for their two small children. She also shared her dream with her parents, hoping Bruce would have the support he would need in a new relationship instead of feeling guilty, remaining alone forever, and allowing her children to grow up without the daily embrace of a loving mother.

This type of open discussion can prevent hostility for your loved ones because people's opinions vary and you might be surprised by their expectations, your daughter included. If she knows your wishes, a lot of freedom can result.

Consider this type of discussion with your family. It was a very selfless thing Terrilynn did that led to incredible healing of her husband and children, and continued celebration of her life. She had the faith to believe that God would answer her prayer and took the appropriate steps to honor her commitment to her hope.

Not long after Terrilynn passed, Bruce met Myra. They soon married. Their story is worthy of a book in itself and, today, in part because of the loving and supportive foundation Terrilynn set in motion, Bruce, Myra, and their two beautiful children live happily. Knowing that they live with Terrilynn's blessing has freed everyone, and has allowed the children to feel the love of a mother again.

This is a powerful and loving gift of life that only you can offer your loved ones. Terrilynn's goodness lives, even in this book, but more importantly, in the heart of her children. You can do the same.

If I Had More Time I Would…..

<u>If Only I had More Time</u> is a normal feeling when we want a re-do in life. Too often there is no re-do, but with the gift of time, you have the opportunity to write about it now.

16

What you get Back.

YOUR LEGACY LIVES ON
THROUGH YOUR DAUGHTER

You may never see the positive and powerful impact you have made -- or maybe you will. Regardless, we know that a loving and caring father who can communicate his wise and impactful thoughts to his child changes her life for the better – forever.

You are a loving father and you have shared with your daughter the most intimate parts of yourself and your life so she can learn to be confident, make smart life choices and, ultimately, lead a happy, fulfilled life. Please know this is not only what you have given your daughter – it goes beyond her into future generations.

You chose to take a step in building your relationship with your daughter through letters, just in case you can't be there with her for whatever reason. But, while you were thinking about and planning your letters, you did something even greater.

You set into motion a positive plan for her life. All of the good and worthwhile plans you wrote about are available. She now has every opportunity to live from a perspective of love and support. She can feel confident and capable because you, her father, told her that she IS loved, IS loveable, IS thought about, and IS special.

She believes you, and she should.

She knows that when she makes a mistake, she can find a life lesson in it and move forward with more information and better strategies. You have told her so.

You taught her and you backed that lesson with your own history and words of wisdom.

She has the courage to jump further toward the dreams that are in her heart, and she is able to step out of her comfort zone to do what's right, or do what's right for her.

She will approach the negative things that happen in her life with positive self-esteem and she will embrace circumstances more readily. She is able to recognize things that alert her to a change that is coming. She will stand up to the experience and use it to climb to the next level with the help and support of your letters.

She will innately teach these powers to her children. Her daughter(s) will grow into emotionally healthier women; her son(s) will grow into emotionally healthier men.

All this because you were brave enough to face your life, to be with your daughter using *The Envelope System*, to prepare her for her very best life.

Thank you very much for helping to shape our world! Your outreach, love, and time contribute to everything that is good in your girl's life and in the life of others. You are a true hero!

ACKNOWLEDGMENTS

My heartfelt gratitude to all of the following:

Luke Anderson, Tracy Arndt, Mary K Bishop, Carol Bush,
Dianne Campbell, Charles Clarage, Ginger Cozzens, Mike Klingler,
Robyn Linn, Dan Lyons, Karen Mainard, Julie Paulson,
Denise Roman, Kathy Rondeau, Shelly Schurr, Michelle Smith,
Steve Strother, and Laurie Wheeler
For your friendship and inspiration.

Debra Anderson, Janice Lizbeth, Kathy and Ruby Mansbridge,
Bruce and Myra Rasku, Tanja and Craig Schneider
For sharing your loved ones with us. Your story brings us hope.

My family, for the experiences we share.
What we know can change the world and we always
get to decide how. Thank you for your influence.

Additional recognition to the following for the drive to force me
deep to my core values and connecting me with the people who
saw in me something I learned to see in myself.
With much gratitude to
The School of Online Business and Coaching Cognition.

Dan, Tori, and Mathias
You shine all that is good in the world.
I am *completely* in love with you.
Hey... Psst...

BIBLIOGRAPHY

Ferguson, E. D. (1984). Adlerian Theory: An Introduction. Chicago: Adler School of Professional Psychology.

Hill, Napoleon Internet.

Kamins, M. L., and Dwerk, C.S. (1999). Person Versus Process Praise and Criticism: Implications for Contingent Self-Worth and Coping. Developmental Psychology, Vol. 35, No. 3, 835-847.

Krohn, F.B., and Bogan, Z. (Dec. 2001). The Effects Absent Fathers Have on Female Development and College Attendance. *College Student Journal,* 35(4), 598. Maslow, A.H. (1943). A Theory of Human Motivation. *Psychological Review*.

Nielsen, L. (March 2007). College Daughters' Relationships With Their Fathers: A 15 year study. Wake Forest University. *College Student Journal, 41*(1), 112-121.

Norment, L., and Chappell, K. (June 2003). Parenting: How Parents Influence the Way Sons and Daughters View Their Dates, Spouses and the World. *Ebony, 58*(8), 35.
Roper Poll (2004). Dads Talk About Their Daughters. NY: United Business Media.

UNIFEM (2010). The Facts: Violence Against Women & Millennium Development Goals.

ABOUT THE AUTHOR

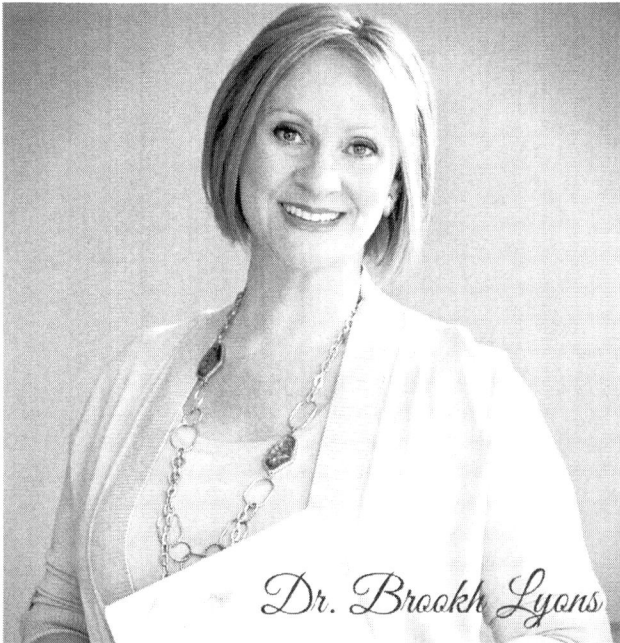

Dr. Brookh Lyons

Brookh Lyons, D.C. is a Board Certified Chiropractor, trained at Palmer College of Chiropractic. She is passionate about the health and wellbeing of children, and families, including the influence of childhood on our decisions into adulthood.

In addition to patient care, Brookh was the publisher of three parenting magazines with a mission to provided support and ideas that inspire parents and caregivers to connect with their children more powerfully. She and her husband, Dan, parent their two children with love and attention to develop their uniqueness, self-care and responsibility. Brookh serves on the Board Of Encompass Early Education and Care, Inc., and as a Health Expert, Mentor Mom, and Teacher in the community.

20806965R00086

Made in the USA
Middletown, DE
10 June 2015